To Lorraine, most steadfast,
loyal and "oldest" friend with
love from Rosi

Grand Tours and the Great War

C. A. Brannen Series

January 1.

First — how I came to be here
after my four or five months travel
abroad. The last two months of
my tour I knew — or rather had
decided to stay for the winter in
Germany. It is needless to say, how
ever, what a trial it was
to come to such a conclusion,
but Brother, as usual came
in at the final moment to insure
that I take any opportunity of
improve myself... It was in Florence
almost at the close of my trip
that, still without any definite
place to break myself in — that
I met Alice McFarland of
Hamilton — and she, I suppose, is
the direct cause of my being
at Mommsen Str. 2, Charlottenburg.
The way she got into France on the
evening before we were to travel and
so accidentally came to our hotel, in
fact, how she got Mrs. Cranberry's address
during our visit to Berlin — the whole
thing is absolutely strange — for Alice
had gotten her facts a little mixed.
But, for that, though, I shouldn't be here.
I wrote right away to Mrs. Cranberry,

Grand Tours
and the Great War

Ima Hogg's Diaries
1907–1918

EDITED WITH COMMENTARY BY
Virginia Bernhard and
Roswitha Wagner

TEXAS A&M UNIVERSITY PRESS
COLLEGE STATION

∞ This paper meets the requirements of ANSI/NISO Z39.48-1992
(Permanence of Paper).
Binding materials have been chosen for durability.
Manufactured in the United States of America

Library of Congress Cataloging-in-Publication Data

Names: Hogg, Ima, author. | Bernhard, Virginia, 1937– editor. | Wagner,
    Roswitha, editor, translator.
Title: Grand tours and the Great War : Ima Hogg's diaries, 1907–1918 /
    edited with commentary, Virginia Bernhard and Roswitha Wagner.
Other titles: C.A. Brannen series.
Description: First edition. | College Station : Texas A&M University Press,
    [2022] | Series: C. A. Brannen series | Includes bibliographical
    references and index.
Identifiers: LCCN 2022016260 | ISBN 9781648431029 (hardcover) | ISBN
    9781648431036 (ebook)
Subjects: LCSH: Hogg, Ima—Diaries. | Hogg, Ima—Travel—Europe. | Children
    of governors—Texas—Diaries. | Women travelers—Texas—Diaries. | World
    War, 1914–1918—Personal narratives, American. | Europe—Description and
    travel. | Europe—Intellectual life—20th century. | LCGFT: Diaries.
Classification: LCC F394.H853 H64 2022 | DDC 976.4/06092
    [B]—dc23/eng/20220429
LC record available at https://lccn.loc.gov/2022016260

Book illustrations from Ima Hogg Papers, courtesy Dolph Briscoe
Center for American History, The University of Texas at Austin.

Cover: Photograph of Ima Hogg, from author's collection. Photograph of the
ship, President Lincoln, was commissioned in May 1907. In June, Ima Hogg was
a passenger on its maiden voyage to Europe. The ship was seized by American
forces during the World War, used as a troop transport, and then sunk by a
German submarine in May 1918. Courtesy of US Army.

Back cover: Photograph courtesy of Dolph Briscoe Center for American History,
The University of Texas at Austin.

Contents

Preface

BY THE TIME she was nine years old, her name was a national joke. The little girl born in Mineola, Texas, in 1882 was known in newspapers coast to coast. According to the San Francisco *Daily Evening Bulletin* on May 2, 1891, "Governor Hogg of Texas named one of his daughters Ima Hogg. Her reproach to her father must be, 'you're another.'"

The *Atchison* (Kansas) *Daily Globe* reported on May 5, 1891: "Governor Hogg, of Texas, has three bright children, two girls and a boy, whose names respectively are said to be Ima Hogg, Ura Hogg and Moore Hogg. These names were bestowed by Governor Hogg himself." Yes, it was Ima's father who named her. No, she did not have siblings named Ura and Moore.

When the editor of the *Chicago Record* wrote to Ima's father in 1896, asking about his children's names, Governor Hogg replied: "I beg to advise you that the names of my children are William, Ima, Mike and Tom—three boys and one girl—whose ages are, respectively, 21, 14, 11, and 9 years."[1]

James Stephen Hogg was a charismatic governor of Texas from 1891 to 1895. Why did he name his only daughter Ima Hogg? There are many stories, and the truth will likely never be known. But that daughter, by the time of her death at ninety-three in 1975, was known all over Texas—and in fact, all over the nation.

Ima Hogg was a philanthropist, a preservationist, an art collector, and a talented musician who made her long life a celebration of the arts. She was a gifted pianist, a graceful dancer, an excellent horsewoman. Her accomplishments would fill several pages—but not in this book.[2] This is about the young Ima, pretty, wealthy, and keenly intelligent, and the diaries she kept. Four of her diaries and a notebook have remained tucked away, largely unused by researchers, in the archives of the Dolph Briscoe Center for American History at the University of Texas at Austin. Transcribed and edited, they appear together in print for the first time.

There are joy and wonder in these diaries and, at the last, sadness. There are clues to mysteries here, but the truth, like the origin of Ima Hogg's name, may never be known. At least half a dozen young men fell in love with her. She saved certain letters. She may have destroyed others. She left gaps in her diaries. She tore out pages. She crossed out others. In later life, she said that she never wanted her biography written.

In 1907 Ima Hogg, age twenty-five, toured England, Scotland, Germany, and Italy from June to October. She kept a richly detailed diary, recording every place, museum, statue, and painting she saw. But in August she impulsively left her travel group and spent ten days by herself in Munich. She took a room in a pension, visiting museums and attending operas. In September she rejoined her touring party but did not return home with them. Ima Hogg had suddenly decided to stay in Germany. She ended her travel diary abruptly in Florence, Italy, on October 4.

On January 1, 1908, Ima began a new diary. On the opening page she wrote her new address: "Berlin, Germany 1908, Mommsenstr. 22, Charlottenburg." On the next page, she wrote, "First, how I came to be here after my four or five months travel abroad." A chance meeting with a Houston friend traveling in Florence had led to Ima's correspondence with another Houston friend then living in Germany about a place to stay in Berlin. On October 10, 1907, Ima arrived in Berlin, met by Leola Fisher, age twenty-two; her younger brother Henry, eighteen; and their sixty-eight-year-old German grandmother, Selma White. Ima would live with them for a year until she sailed for home in October 1908. As for Ima's sudden desire to live in Berlin, she wrote, "I was most anxious to learn to speak German—more than to take up my music, really." Why was she so eager to learn German?

In her diary, Ima wrote almost every day of her adventures in Charlottenburg, an affluent suburb of Berlin. Her little diary has a lock and key. Who was the intended audience? Ima wrote of the concerts and operas she attended, of books read, games of checkers played, German lessons, and piano lessons. She studied with noted teachers. She rejected a suitor, Charles Scott, one of her 1907 travel companions. He had wooed her on their tour and pursued her in Berlin, but she did not reveal his proper name in the 1908 diary. She called him "Areal."

After Charles Scott, Ima's 1908 diary does not mention any other suitors. Ima Hogg was pretty, talented, and vivacious. In Berlin, in a milieu of young people studying music, did no young men pay court to her? Did she have a secret romance? Was this the reason she wanted so much to become fluent in German and to stay in Germany?

After February 29, 1908, with no explanation, Ima stopped writing in her diary. Her reasons for ending the diary and her activities for much of this time are unrecorded. Ima spent part of that summer vacationing in the Harz Mountains with the Fishers: Leola, Henry, their grandmother, and Leola's parents. Ima returned to Berlin and sailed for home on October 12, 1908. Once again in Houston, she resumed the life she had led, attending parties and visiting friends in Austin. She also began teaching piano, mentoring a select group of students.

In 1910 Ima Hogg sailed again for Europe, this time with her brother Mike. She used the remaining pages of her 1907 travel diary to record their time in Germany, Belgium, and England. As before, when touring, she wrote details of each place she and Mike visited—hotels, meals, museums—but the twelve days they spent in Berlin are not recorded.

Ima returned again to Germany in 1912, traveling with two young women friends. If she kept a diary this time, it has not been found. In 1914 she went back to Germany, arriving on August 1, just as World War I was about to begin. Ima and other passengers who had sailed on the German liner *Chemnitz* were not allowed to remain in Germany. Relocated to London on August 3, Ima began a daily journal, which she kept until September 15, when she was at last able to book passage on a ship bound for New York. As she recorded news of the Great War that fateful summer, her sentiments were decidedly pro-German. They always were.

Here, a bit of hearsay: A longtime friend of Ima's, reminiscing after Ima's death in 1975, remarked, "Every time she went to Europe, she always went to Germany." Docents at Bayou Bend (Ima's former home, now the Bayou Bend Collection of the Museum of Fine Arts, Houston) talked of rumors that Ima had had a romance in Germany with a young man who was killed in World War I. As the story went, Ima destroyed all of his letters, but she kept in touch with his family and always visited them when she went to Germany. None of this can be proved. Ima's 1918 notebook adds to the mystery.

In the summer of 1918 Ima Hogg took a little notebook with her as she vacationed in New York, Pennsylvania, and New England. She wrote at the top of the first page: "Summer 1918." On that page is a list of addresses of antiques dealers. Ima was looking for furnishings for a house; one page of her notebook is a rough sketch of a floor plan. She also made notes for research she hoped to do on symphony orchestras in other cities. (Ima had been elected president of the Houston Symphony that spring.) Suddenly, halfway through the notebook, she copied out a handful of contemporary poems about war and tragic deaths in battle. What had happened?

In the summer of 1918, from June 2 to June 26, the great Battle of Belleau Wood raged, with devastating German losses. Every day's newspapers trumpeted the news. Ima could not have avoided seeing the stark banner headlines. Could she have received a cablegram or letter from Germany, telling her news she dreaded to hear?

In early July 1918, not long after her thirty-sixth birthday on July 10, Ima Hogg became ill. She suffered what would later be called a nervous breakdown. Her notebook contains five pages with a large black "X" across each page, five pages of lists of antique furniture and artworks. Some pages have been neatly cut off. Others are torn out. For much of the autumn of 1918 Ima Hogg was in an exclusive retreat "for overworked people" in the mountains of Upstate New York. For the next three years, 1919 to 1922, she was under the care of a noted Philadelphia specialist in mental health. In April 1923 Ima, fully recovered, and Will and Mike took a celebratory trip to Europe. Will sailed home in June; Mike, in July. Ima did not come home until August.

All her long life, Ima Hogg was very good at keeping secrets. Readers of this book may draw their own conclusions.

Acknowledgments

This book has been long in the making, and a great many people helped. First of all, thanks to the Dolph Briscoe Center for American History at The University of Texas for permission to publish Ima Hogg's diaries and selected photographs from the Ima Hogg Papers. The staff, especially Margaret Schlankey, head of reference services; and Aryn Glazier, duplication services, were unfailingly helpful. Thanks also go to the *Southwestern Historical Quarterly* for permission to publish Ima Hogg's World War I diary, which appeared as "Ima Hogg in Europe, 1914: A Texan Experiences the Beginning of the Great War," *SHQ* 119, no. 3 (January 2016).

Thanks also go to the staff at the Museum of Fine Arts, Houston archives, and to Margaret Culbertson at the Bayou Bend Collection. For her continued interest in this project, Bonnie Campbell, director of Bayou Bend, deserves a vote of thanks, along with Jeanne Jaard, the owner of the River Oaks Bookstore. Conversations with Jeanne were the inspiration for this book. Without the helpful staffs at the Clayton Library for Genealogical Research and the University of Houston's Anderson Library, Special Collections, the background narrative for the diaries would be much thinner.

Colleagues who read, advised, and consulted were Paula Baker, Ryan Schumacher, Kate Kirkland, and Carl Cunningham. We want to thank Patricia Clabaugh and Cynthia Lindlof at Texas A&M University Press for their diligence and patience.

We thank our husbands, Jim Bernhard and Harrison Wagner, for their patience in listening to our endless discussions about Ima Hogg.

—Virginia Bernhard and Roswitha Wagner
November 2021

NOTE ON SOURCES

IMA HOGG'S DIARIES are in the Ima Hogg Papers at the Dolph Briscoe Center for American History at the University of Texas at Austin. They have been transcribed and edited for this book. Punctuation and spelling have been corrected for clarity's sake. Ellipses indicate omitted passages of extraneous material—detailed descriptions of paintings, sculptures, and museum exhibits, for example, that can be found in any guidebook.

an... [illegible]... Mrs. Granberry is from Houston. I had known her slightly there, through friends, — quite well. So I thought it might be nice to stay in the place with her, at least until I could find a German family to live with. I was most anxious to learn to speak German — more than to take up my Music really. — Well, by the time I got back to Florence I shall an answer to my letter from Mrs. C. She was most cordial and told me that they weren't exactly what would be apprehensive, but that there was a room for me. In the middle of October I bade my dear friends good-bye and started out on my journey all alone and awfully lonesome, too. The following night I arrived in B. And what started me off in B. just right — my things welcomed at the station by Mrs. C. and her Brother. Fräser was at Savigny Platz to welcome me there. I went the next morning, when I was tired and homesick, and wondering really what I was going to do here — the Merchant came in and told me that they were going

Grand Tours and the Great War

Figure 1. Ima Hogg, ca. 1900

1

~~ԚԸ~~

The Grand Tour

EUROPE, 1907

AS THE SUMMER of 1907 began, Ima Hogg was twenty-four years old. It had been more than a year since her father's death, and the only daughter of James Stephen Hogg was still in mourning for him. Her mother had died of tuberculosis when Ima was thirteen, and Ima had become, as her father said, "the sunshine of my household." She attended the University of Texas at Austin from 1899 to 1901, but after completing two years there she went off to New York to pursue one of her lifelong passions: music. Already a gifted pianist, she studied at the National Conservatory of Music from 1901 to 1903. An injury to her knee and family obligations ended Ima's New York sojourn, but not before she had savored the delights of concerts and operas in that city.

In 1905 Ima's father suffered an injury in a train accident, and she became his nurse and constant companion until he died suddenly of heart failure in March 1906. Ima was devastated. She found solace in visits to friends in New York and Austin, in playing her piano, and in taking her Arabian horse, Napoleon, for drives around Houston, but she was still sad and restless. Her older brother, Will, then in his thirties and now head of the family, worried about her. So did the younger brothers, Mike and Tom. Then a Houston friend, Mrs. Lewis Thompson, planning a tour of Europe with her family, invited Ima to join them. Ima now had money of her own: A special bequest in Jim Hogg's will had left her at least seven thousand dollars, about two hundred thousand dollars in present-day purchasing power.[1]

Ima had traveled abroad with her father to Mexico and Hawaii, but this would be her first trip to Europe, an extensive tour that would last from June to October. It began on June 22, 1907, when she and her travel companions sailed from New York on a transatlantic steamship bound for Plymouth, England. On that day Ima began her diary in a small black leather-bound journal.[2]

Figure 2. 1907 diary

> This is to be a Chronicle of my trip to Europe and not a diary of
> personalities. June 22—Sailing—President Lincoln, Hamburg-
> American
> An auspicious start—a glorious warm day, our ship—618 ft.
> long—making its maiden trip.

The *President Lincoln* of the Hamburg-American line would come to a
sad end: Seized by the United States in New York during World War I,
it was converted to a transport vessel and sunk by a German submarine
on May 31, 1918.[3]

> Many friends had telegrams, letters, books and flowers as farewell
> to us, and we waved them a far away good-bye with grateful hearts
> for their remembrances—a home leaving being at best somewhat
> sad. Mr. Scott, Professor of Chemistry in Austin College, Sherman,
> Texas; Mr. Ben Foster and his sister, Miss Ione [Foster] of Kansas
> City—joined the original party which consisted of Mr. & Mrs. Lewis
> Thompson, Magdalene the governess with little Ben & Lewis—all of
> us from Houston and Mrs. Ben Thompson of Nacogdoches, Texas.

Ima was sailing with a group whose members were some years older than
she, and she referred to them as "Mr." and "Mrs." in her diary. Lewis
and Helen Thompson, both thirty-two, were wealthy Houstonians. Their
sons, Lewis Jr. and Ben, were "little" indeed: they were four and three.
Evidently their parents did not wish to travel abroad without them,
hence their "governess," Magdalene, was more like a nanny. Ima's cabin
mate, Mrs. Ben (Lucy) Thompson, was a forty-one-year-old widow.
Her husband, Ben, Lewis's brother, had died in 1896. Charles Scott
was a forty-year-old bachelor and college professor (he had been voted
"handsomest" faculty member of Austin College in 1906). Benjamin
Foster, forty-four, and his sister, Ione, thirty-two, may have known the
Thompsons through professional contacts: Thompson and Foster had
both made fortunes in the lumber business. All together, they made up
a travel group of ten.[4] They would be abroad from June to October, when
all but two sailed for home: Charles Scott, as he had planned, stayed for
a year of study at the University of Heidelberg. Ima Hogg impulsively
decided to live in Berlin for the winter.

Ima had had no idea of doing such a thing when this trip began. As she wrote in her diary aboard the ship, "Shuffle-board is a great game—I can't play it much, but intend to spend lots of time at it on the return." But Ima Hogg did not return as planned. She wrote in the new diary she began in Berlin on January 1, 1908: "The last two months of my tour, I knew or rather had decided to stay for the winter in Germany. . . . I was most anxious to learn to speak German. . . ." Before that, on the way to Europe, Ima Hogg enjoyed life at sea.

> Much of our time has been spent at cards, some at reading: we have been dutiful enough to dive into guide-books—then we've walked leagues. . . . And the weather continued just temperate until two days ago then became stormy and very cold—all happened just to my taste. I shall not begin to describe the never ceasing fascination of the sea, and the moonlit nights—as well as the sunset of last evening, but I shall remember them always. No one has been sea-sick—the credit due to our perfect sailing ship. Tomorrow we expect to reach Plymouth where we shall bid a reluctant good-bye to our ship.

From July 22, 1907, when Ima and her companions went ashore at Plymouth, England, to their last stop in Florence, Italy, in October, she wrote in her diary nearly every day. She obviously felt the need to make her diary, as she said, "a Chronicle" of everything she saw. Her descriptions of statues, paintings, and buildings often read like a guidebook, but her descriptions of adventures with her travel companions and her impressions of places reveal a sense of humor and a keen intellect.

> *July 1, Plymouth*
> At about ten o'clock A.M., sighted <u>Plymouth</u>. Got in about 11:15 and the first sight which greeted us was [a] "Pear's Soap" advertisement! Mr. Thompson & Mr. Foster stayed with the luggage at the Customs House, & Mr. Scott escorted us in dumpy "four wheelers" over the cobblestones so that we created a distinctly embarrassing feeling of disturbance through the quiet quaint old streets. . . . Spent the night at the <u>Royal</u>—a fair hotel with single room with comfortable beds at 5 shillings. We were roused at 6:30 A.M. in order to breakfast & catch the 8:30 train for Salisbury.

July 2, Salisbury and Winchester

Mr. Foster's report of going through Customs officials inspection simply killing. Seems there was a good deal of red tape, much tipping—there having been in attendance of them all the loafers around the dock—got through after $14.50 tips in small fees. Mr. F. says that of all the people there he & Mr. T. "had the biggest crowd." They are sore with us women this morning for owning so much luggage.

On the train to Salisbury Ima wrote:

What can I say to express my delight with rural England! The cozy little compartment, the tiny engines, etc. so novel & fun to us. The country houses & the style of architecture in the perfectly kept range of small farms, the flowers, the hedges instead of fences. At the first station a small boy passed our window with a tray of strawberries. For 6 d. we got a tiny paper basket with at least 1½ doz. tremendous berries all daintily nested in fresh green leaves, with a little envelope labeled "sugar" to go with it, and they were so sweet themselves, we hardly needed to dip them in the sugar. We made one change before reaching Salisbury. After a refreshing & simple lunch—proceeded to the Cathedral in two queer equipages, like our very old-fashioned "hacks," though these heavy things are drawn by one horse only. The Cathedral is my first great one, & I am overwhelmed by its symmetry and beauty of exterior, though even the quiet bare interior is most uplifting & inspiring. . .

Left for Winchester at 3:15 P.M. Several changes. Lots of fun carrying our own bags. I have <u>two</u> & my rugs. Decided to come to the <u>Royal Hotel</u>—here in Winchester—rambling bus down narrow quaintest streets we've seen—to this charming old inn with its walled-vined-in well-laid-out formal garden at the side of the house. I am sitting in the cozy inn parlor now looking out at the twilight just settling down on it. . . . Mrs. Thompson and I have a room together for 5 shillings—2/6 each. Late this afternoon Mr. Scott took us to view the outside of the Cathedral here. . . .

This is Ima's first of several excursions with Charles Scott, the handsome bachelor and college professor.

> We walked through the close gate passing the Bishop's palace—or Deanery—& most lovely houses with high walls, so old the mosses & weeds grow on top. Of all the pretty sights to me, the avenue leading to the Cathedral is sweetest. . . . Tomorrow we are saving for the view inside the church. By the way, maids, candles, service is extra, about 16 sh. altogether, dinner was 4/6 table d'hôte. The old-timey bell ropes in the rooms, the funny tubs under the dressing-table are indicative of some age.

> *July 3, London*
> Refer myself for details to Baedeker![5] It seems irreverent for curious eyes to gaze at this solemn monument to the genius of so many ages of religious feeling—It makes one feel like a barbarian to find you've walked over the resting place of Jane Austen. . . . I had many thrills to find myself near the tombs of the great as long back as the 11th century! I believe for the first time I know what History means! It was bitterly cold in the church, raining outside, so I dared not linger afterwards as I longed to do.—We took a hurried drive just before the train left to see the Winchester Hall, which they claim to have King Arthur's round table. We passed a tiny little house, too, where Jane Austen lived. . . .

> *July 4, London*
> Arrived yesterday morning with much the same feeling as approaching N.Y.—Don't care for the City—yet. Although I am longing to get into Westminster & the Art Galleries. Spent this day loafing—all of us tired.

Ima may have been tired, but she was fearless about venturing out by herself in a strange city.

> Went to Cook, got an umbrella & felt my way about all alone in town. Lunched at a queer place—just anywhere—and found my companions of the cab driver class! Nice things to eat, but interested

to find them eating with a fork & spoon—did not give me a knife! Came home to find Mrs. Thompson had box seats for the Opera at Covent Garden.

Ima does not say whether this Mrs. Thompson was her roommate, Lucy, or her Houston friend, Helen. The latter would become one of Ima's closest friends.

Dressed in our much wrinkled finery, but after we were there— who cared? Caruso & Melba with a good cast gave us La Bohème (Puccini's). . . . The tier after tier of boxes were filled with coronets and handsome gowns, few lovely faces. The Royal Box had two hideous very ordinary women in it. . . .

July 5, London
John Smith's burial at a church near Pie Street, the immensely interesting Tower. . . . Saw the place where the people were beheaded outside the Towers then the little church where they were usually buried. . . . These English are a never ending source of wonder. For the first time I am thoroughly at home with all the characters we read of. They are not to be found anywhere else on every side as they are here. I more than ever appreciate Dickens. Such expressions as "at the top of the street," the car on top (ahead), banking office (ticket office)—I can't always tell an Eng. from a Frenchman speaking broken Eng.!

July 6, London
Parliament this morning at ten-thirty. A mob in it so we were pushed rapidly through. It is all very rich in decoration but saved from being too gaudy by the beauty. The Westminster Hall is the oldest & by far the grandest. . . . Here we saw the spot on which Charles II stood for trial. Westminster Abbey is superb inside. . . .
We next went to the Tate Gallery. . . .

July 7, London
Church at St. Paul's. Acoustics miserable. Miss Foster & I left the men Mr. F., Mr. S., & Mr. T. & saw the wonderful sight at Hyde

Park—the Church Parade. Very beautiful women, magnificently
gowned, & I adore the Eng. men in their top hats. Lunched very
fashionably after at the Berkeley on the Park. Came home & rested
all the rest of the day.

July 8, London

Shopped at Peter Robinson's & down Regent Street. Lunch at
Stewart's Bond & Piccadilly—lovely place. National Gallery in the
afternoon. . . .

July 9, London

Tate Gallery . . . Put on a voile gown . . . thin yoke,—sneezed & knew
a cold was coming.

July 10, London

Windsor Castle. Drove over—coached to Windsor—Left our
trunks—two apiece!—at the hotel, taking only suitcases for our tour
up through Scotland. . . . Started at 10:30 got to Windsor 2:30.
St. George's Chapel with Princess Charlotte monument & Henry
VIII burial place. White Tower where the Order of the Garter
organized, building in which Merry Wives of Windsor was first
played. Then the beautiful view towards Eton from the steps—
where I turned my ankle & scrambled up by Mr. Scott's coat sleeves.
Dreadfully caught more cold.

July 10 was Ima Hogg's twenty-fifth birthday. Did she keep this a secret
from her companions? She does not mention her birthday in her diary.

July 11, Oxford

Real sick but ambitious in such a spot. . . . Oxford is very quaint
with its high walls & old architecture—We drove by all the points
of interest—stopping next at New College for a walk in its exquisite
gardens walled in by the ancient city walls. . . . Mrs. Thompson,
Mrs. B.T., Mr. Foster, & Miss F. all drove to Blenheim castle—the
rest of us [Ima, Lewis Thompson, and Charles Scott] preferring
to stay in Oxford. After lunch went back to Christ C. & into the

Cathedral. . . . Sunny beautiful day so we lingered along the shady path running towards Magdalen. This is the sweetest of all the colleges, I think. We didn't go inside the buildings here but in the quadrangles through the cloisters, on the bridge where the swans—black ones—swim, into the Addison Walk! . . . How I long to get back to Oxford, once again.

Arrived at Warwick—7—leaving 5:55 P.M.—in time to view from the Bridge over the Avon the picturesque castle. It does not get dark here, anyhow, until after <u>nine</u>.

July 12, Warwick

"Warwick Arms." <u>Very poor</u>.

All morning in Castle & the grounds. Walk cut through stone—wonderful. Leaning trees high above, vines, etc. Peacocks everywhere. . . . Drove over late in the afternoon to Stratford-on-Avon. . . . The crowd think they have a good joke on me. Hopped out to pick some poppies & fell into a ditch—Mr. Foster & Mr. Scott were frightened to death & ran to pick me up. Laughed all the rest of the afternoon at the picture, me with the umbrella only in view. Reached Stratford sick, but walked to Trinity and out by the Avon—my only chance for I spent July 13—Stratford-on-Avon—in bed.

After a day of rest, Ima's cold was better, and she resumed her sightseeing.

July 14, Stratford

Walked to Anne Hathaway's cottage. V. Romantic pathway. Rowed on the Avon this afternoon. . . . Saw Shakespeare's birthplace & where his home used to be. . . . Sorry to miss so much on account of illness as we leave in the morning at 9:30.

July 15, Chester 1:45, Liverpool 5:00

Chester the scene of Orangemen celebration—Everybody decorated in orange ribbons—gala costumes. . . . Good to reach an up to date hotel with electric light & elevator. Candles & winding stairs trying on too long a stretch.

July 16, Liverpool
Hotel Adelphi very good, reasonable. Walker Art Gallery . . . Took train at 11:10 for the <u>English Lakes</u>.

July 16, Grasmere
Beautiful situation. Hotel Prince of Wales good & cheap. Lakeside station at 1:41—had lunch in basket brought on at Lancaster where from the train we saw the beautiful old castle. From there on mountains were wonderfully beautiful. . . . Took boat at Lakeside, and enjoyed a trip on the Windermere as far as Waterhead, where we coached five miles to this delightful spot. Has gotten warmer, the sun is bright, the mountains clear yet the soft enveloping haze on them is velvety and gives a gorgeous color to the dark places. . . . Rowed on the lake after dinner with Mr. Scott. Going back to the drive after settling ourselves for a stay at this hotel. Drove on, past the little church where lie Wordsworth & Southey. Nearby is the rock over the lake where Wordsworth loved to dream. They say if you sit there five minutes you get up either a poet or a fool. I <u>may</u> try it. Is twelve miles to Coniston & nobody wants the journey!

July 17, Grasmere
Read all morning. Late spell [Ima's cold] not over yet. But after lunch took the stage—passing Coleridge's home—and went to the rock overlooking Rydal Water & read Wordsworth's Ode on Immortality, The Nightingale, The Daisy, Duty, etc. Mr. Scott went with me and read a little of Ruskin on Happiness, Economy, & other bits. In such a spot, I felt a keener appreciation for . . . the two men's thoughts than I should ever elsewhere. . . . After dinner played by the lovely window & watched the sun go down. Have just come from fishing—a dear small boy had worms, so he helped me, also to lose the only fish which bit!! Is now 9:45 & still twilight!

Ima Hogg knew how to bait a hook: She grew up with three brothers and a father who loved to fish. So did she. She does not say if others in her party went fishing with her that day. "Before leaving went through Dove Cottage. Saw DeQuincy's room & Wordsworth's bed."

July 18, Coniston—Furness Abbey

Twelve miles of the most beautiful scenery! Passed by our old
friends the rock, Rydal Mount, on to the sight of Ambleside, by
the Stepping Stones, past Dr. Arnold's, Miss Martineau's over
in the distance to the left. Lots of fun all the way. The spirit has
gone into us all, even Mr. F. talking of babbling brooks, & "purple
hazes"! Visited Ruskin's modest resting place—neglected-looking
churchyard. . . . Walked over the bridge & bought a little volume of
his work. Lunched at Waterhead Hotel—the best lunch yet in Eng.—
wonderful cream cheese. By boat to [left blank] where the men had
to lug in all the luggage up a big hill. Coached to Greenodd—took
train for Furness Abbey. Never saw anything more fascinating . . .
such tremendous Norman Arches & beautiful proportions. The
hotel is within the gates, and there we dined. Sailed on a miserable
boat from Barrow to Belfast Ireland—8:30 P.M.

July 19, Belfast

Grand Central—Bad fare. (Visited market 2:30 P.M.) Got off boat at
8:30 A.M. took a ride over the dirty ugly place in a jaunting-cart—
riding facing out—over the two wheels. Nice riding. Didn't find
much [in] bargains, though. Very good values in linens & laces. . . .
Back on boat at 8:30 for Glasgow.

July 20, Glasgow

Breakfast at Glasgow, Grand Central. Drove to St. Mungo's
Cathedral. . . . Arrived by train in the Scottish Lake District at
Bulloch. Took steamer on Loch Lomond to Inversnaid, coached
to Stronachlacher Hotel, Loch Katrine, vaster & wilder than Eng.
Lakes, only very hazy today. On road—train passed the castle
Dumbarton of "Scottish Chiefs" fame. "Lady of the Lake" is the
story of the lake on which we are located till Monday. Went out in
a boat fishing with trolling line & minnow "fake bait" & caught a
pretty little trout! Mr. Scott was along & didn't get a bite. [Ima, the
skilled fisherman, was amused enough by Charles Scott's lack of
success to note it in her diary.] Bought two copies of Lady of Lake
on boat on the Lake later.

July 21, Inversnaid

Sunday—All went by coach to Inversnaid Presbyterian Church
along the Arklet water. Nice service & unusually good sermon.
"Seek ye first the Kingdom of God." . . . Coming back, took
occasion to notice the sheep with wool of 30 lbs. weight, a shepherd
informed us. Read Lady of the Lake in the afternoon looking out
on Loch Katrine. After dinner all started out for a little walk,
but went on & on until we reached the water system for Glasgow,
some 2 ½ miles at least from the hotel—the walk back was nice—
5 miles, though, after a long day! Gathered heather along the steep
mountain climbs, but the heather is not in good bloom until the
"back of the month"—so a Scot informs us.

July 22, Stirling

Early rising.—6:30—took steam boat for the Trossach Landing in
front of Ellen's Isle. . . . Took train to Stirling, lunched at Golden
Lion—a minute walk from the station, fair place, only. Walked up
the hill to the Castle, & stopped at Grey Friars, pretty old church. . . .
3:20 train for Edinburgh. Went to Old Waverly, but so poor were our
quarters that [we] came to the Carleton which seems to be very nice.
Awfully hungry these days.

July 23, Edinburgh

Walked to St. Giles: bas-relief memorial of Stevenson by Augustus
St. Gaudens. . . . Visited Parliament buildings behind—huge
Assembly Hall with heavy oak ceiling. In front of bldg. stood
existing burial place of John Knox but is said to be removed to
Grey-Friars (?). . . . Wandered down hill past Edinburgh Castle
Rock stronghold & Grass Market. . . .

July 24, Edinburgh

Shampoo this morning. Two o'clock carriage—Mrs. B.T., Mr. Scott
& I—to Roslin Chapel & Castle. Guide was quite flowery then patient
at times describing this "gem" of stone work. . . . Walked down to old
ruined castle. Very picturesque. Drove back by Stevenson's boy-hood
home. . . .

July 25, Edinburgh
Shopping—poor entertainment for a day.

July 26, Edinburgh (Melrose)
10:30 A.M. 11:30 to Melrose. By brake to Abbotsford—Scott's home.
Very grand old place & still well kept up by his granddaughter who
lives there. The tourists are let in the back door together, & we saw
the private rooms, only a few, of Sir Walter's. . . . His little study is
conveniently arranged—a tiny gallery at the top running around
from the small door which led to his bed-room so he could come
down any time of night & write undisturbed. . . .

July 27, London
7:00-4:00 P.M. . . . "When Knights Were Bold," Theatre Wyndham.
Perfectly great. Mr. Foster had gotten tickets. Fitted in perfectly
with our trip—"the good old days"!!

This three-act farce was one of the hit shows in London. A review in the
Daily Mirror on September 14, 1906, describes it:

The play shows the trials of Sir Guy de Vere, who despises his baronetcy,
and is by way of being an amateur Socialist. The second act sees all
the characters, with the exception of Sir Guy, transformed into their
mediæval prototypes. The unhappy baronet is forced into a suit of
armour and a duel, in which he is accidentally successful. After three
acts of furious fun every one is made happy.

That included Ima Hogg and her companions.

July 28-29, London
Nothing Sunday—Monday morning saw Cook about tickets for
Munich, paying £4/8 in advance for them, to be gotten at office
in Munich. National Gallery, seeing Flemish & Dutch painters—
numbering somewhat changed & confusing. My Ward Lock & Co.
[guidebook] quite helpful in visiting gallery.

July 30, London
Resting—

July 31, London—Bruges
Took train at 9:00 for Dover, boat three hours 11:30 to 3:30 Ostend Belgium. Horrid little trip—all of us awfully upset. Belgium rich farming country along route from O. to B.

Aug. 1, Bruges—Brussels
Visit to St. John Hospital to see the Memlings . . . [paintings by the fifteenth-century artist Hans Memling]. These masterpieces are truly worth our trip to Bruges—only it should take longer than the two hours we gave them.

Aug. 2, Brussels (Waterloo)
We saw the Chateau de Hougoumont, in front of it . . . Farm of La Belle Alliance, Napoleon's center of command. . . . The front of the chateau is intact, the walls so thick that only the mark of the bullets to show the fusillade of the French infantry. . . . Hougoumont is [now] used as a filthy chicken ranch. . . .

Aug. 3, Brussels-Antwerp-Hague
Shopped all morning. Rue de la Madeleine most fascinating shopping district I ever saw. . . . Train for Antwerp at 12:55 Midi station, arriving about 2:00. . . . Belgium is a delightful country, seemingly prosperous: great farming country & rows of tall topped trees by every roadside in the country. . . . Left Antwerp for The Hague at 5:55 P.M. arriving at 8:45. Inspector at border line merely came through train & asked us if we had anything to declare. So many speak Eng. we have little trouble. Some fellow travelers in Belgium told Mr. S. that the Americans are coming over in such numbers every year that it wouldn't be long before English would be the universal language, & it wouldn't be "Shakespeare or Spenser, but the American dollar which taught them."! Some holding up in Holland at the hotel when we arrived—the Peace Conference is in session.

The historic Peace Conference of 1907 did not prevent World War I. On another trip, Ima Hogg arrived in Germany just as the Great War began. Her 1914 diary is included in this book.

Aug. 4, The Hague-Amsterdam

Hotel Paulez. In the afternoon by train through wonderful wooded road to Scheveningen—beach & seashore resort. Heard part of lovely orchestra concert—Berlin Philharmonic Orches.—Dutch good looking people.

Aug. 5, The Hague-Amsterdam

To the Royal Art Gallery. . . . Parliament building holds conference meetings now, drove there too. . . . Train at 3:15 P.M. for <u>Amsterdam</u>. Hotel L'Europe, right on a canal. Funny old chimes ring out the quarter hours.

Aug. 6, Amsterdam

"Funny old chimes" kept me awake all night! Excursion to the Isle of Marken on a little steam boat full of Americans. Starting at wharf in harbor went into canal where we were let down into the canal by the lock. Not particularly pretty scenery, but interesting to see the peasants along there, come driving in small carts pulled by dogs going along as cheerily as you please. At Broek in Waterland inspected the cheese making. The people & the cattle all lie together in the winter.

Aug. 7, Cologne

Visited Rijks Gallery. . . . Rembrandt's "Night Watch" is magnificently hung in a perfectly lighted room all by itself. . . . Took train at 11:45 for <u>Cologne</u>. Lack of water all the five or six hrs. almost perished. . . .

Aug. 8, Cologne

Hotel du Nord. Took a guide who showed us the Chapels of the Three Kings. . . . By boat on the Rhine to Coblenz—We took our first German beer.

Aug. 9, Coblenz to Wiesbaden

In morning to Stolzenfels by car, long steep winding, beautiful walk to the Castle. . . . Through the place with a German party— no English—but we managed to catch on to a bit about the room where Victoria spent her honeymoon. . . . The little chapel was quite lovely—also the dining room. The castle now is owned by the crown prince. Took <u>Kaiser Wilhelm</u> at 1:00 up Rhine. . . . The two last days are among my pleasantest in Europe, bright warm days. . . .

Aug. 10-15, Wiesbaden

Hotel Berliner—<u>fair</u>. Beautiful town but have been resting so completely haven't seen a thing but the park by the front and the magnificent Kurhaus across. <u>Music all day</u>. Germany is adorable. Germans kindly and homely.

[August 13]

We had a nice evening at concert by a pianist & violinist at Kurhaus concert hall.

August 14, Frankfurt

Frankfurter Hof good. Warm day, hour's trip reaching there about nine-thirty. From train walked up Kaiser Strasse gazing in fascinating shop windows.

August 15 in Frankfurt is not recorded.

Aug. 16, Heidelberg

Left about 8:30 A.M. reaching H. about 11:15.

Grand Hotel good. Early lunch & <u>walked</u>—took a carriage drive, going along the river & turning beyond bridge up side of hill to the old eating house where it has been the custom for over a hundred years to duel with swords. In a room upstairs . . . the floor is covered with blood stains. The students of Heidelberg meet there now when candidates for any of their clubs (fraternities) successfully fight four men—as soon as blood is drawn the surgeon intervenes. They say fraternities originated in Heidelberg. We then drove across the old bridge, getting a view of the ruined castle. Spent some time after drive walking—finally finding ourselves in the castle. The walk up is tiring but quite worth it along the quaint narrow streets. Were caught in the rain going up & stopped at an inn where delightful lemonade and coffee cake were brought. It is quite too delicate a demand on me to describe the rest of our day—one of the most satisfying I can imagine. . . .

After dinner went for a bit to a band concert.

Aug. 17, Freiburg

Zähringer Hof good. Left Heidelberg about 10:30 A.M. Late lunch at Freiburg about 2:30 P.M.—took carry-all for drive of two hours—4-6. Freiburg extremely quaint—beautiful, surrounded by mountains of the Black Forest. . . .

Aug. 18, Munich

(all day on train) Raining early in morning and until about twelve. Went through tunneled mts.—and the Black Forest. The care of the German government for the lovely forests is great & they have made & kept up roads—a city park all through—in places the tiny trees are growing in perfect rows to replenish the forests. Would that our own Texas had some laws to protect our poor trees. Changed trains at four places. . . .

Tired and glad to reach Munich about 7:15 P.M. tired & awfully hot & hungry.

August 19 in Munich is not recorded.

Aug. 20, Munich

At the Pinakothek [museum] for two or more hours in the morning where I found myself happy & contented. . . .

Aug. 21, Munich

Ima, the opera-lover, attended an opera in Munich. She does not say who, if anyone, accompanied her. "Four o'clock Tristan & Isolde! Started from hotel in carriage at 3:30 in plenty of time. Surprised to find so little dressing." To Ima Hogg, attending an opera meant dressing up. Munich audiences, at least in midweek, were more informal. But the theater itself pleased her.

> A fine, intelligent audience, beautiful Prinz Regent Theatre with large stage. Concealed orchestra. An atmosphere quite equal to this most perfect of Wagner's musical productions. . . . I have heard better all-around singing at the Metropolitan but I was in the right mood. . . . Had dinner and a good one between 2nd and 3rd Acts. . . .

After the performance Ima made a momentous decision: "Came home decided on leaving out Vienna & staying for Cycle—if my ticket could be redeemed." She would leave her tour companions and stay in Munich for Wagner's four-opera Ring Cycle.

[August 22,] Munich

Her mind made up, Ima lost no time. She put her plan into action the very next day.
"Ticket redeemed, place engaged at Quisisana Pension where Mrs. [name left blank] from Houston is staying & she, too, goes to the opera."

When Ima announced her change of plans, Mrs. Lewis Thompson stepped in to help. She knew a friend from Houston (whose name Ima evidently did not remember at first) was staying at the Quisisana, a pension, or boardinghouse, in Munich. The Quisisana is still in existence. A newspaper ad in *T. P.'s Weekly* on July 7, 1905, stated: "A good pension in Munich, quite suitable for ladies is the Quisisana, 83, Theresienstrasse (from 4.50 marks a day)."

As it happened, Ima was not the only one temporarily leaving the tour: "Mr. Scott & Mr. Foster went to St. Petersburg—Mr. Thompson to join them in Berlin Tues. or Wed. morning."

Aug. 23, Munich

Mrs. B.T., Mrs. L.T., & Miss Ione F. waved me farewell on the omnibus at 9 A.M. All alone—but glad I'm not going to Vienna— am sick of improving my mind—don't think I have any—so am going in madly for <u>Wagner & Opera</u>—not too madly for I am really physically, mentally, morally, spiritually and nerve <u>exhausted</u>—

Have just settled my things most permanent-like in a cozy nice
Zimmer [room] at this pension.[6]

There is a wistful note to her use of "most permanent-like." Here Ima
Hogg could pretend she lived in Munich. For the first time in her twenty-
five years, she was on her own in a city where no one knew her. All
her life, whether in Austin or Houston or New York City, she had been
Governor Hogg's daughter. Here in Munich she could be herself. And
here her name did not evoke laughter. In German, the word for "hog"
is "Schwein."

Ima moved into the Quisisana on Friday, August 23, and left there on
September 3, a stay of ten days. She, who usually wrote down everything
she did every day, left several gaps in her Munich diary.

August 24 to [August 28,] Munich
Mrs. Cooper, the friend whom Mrs. Thompson has asked to look
after me is delightful & has taken me in full charge. [This friend
may have been Mary J. Cooper, a wealthy Houston widow.[7]] My
time has been most profitably spent in listening to the discussion of
various scientific and everyday subjects by two men at our table—
Mr. Baumgardt, and Mr. Monroe. And Miss Koerner, studying
for opera, has sung some beautiful von Fielitz songs among other
things, Rubinstein's lovesong (Romance for Piano).[8] We have visited
the new Pinakothek across the street. . . . Also visited the Alte
Pinakothek.

These activities, including the Pinakothek museum visits, were presumably on Saturday and Sunday, August 24 and 25. "On Monday
afternoon [August 26] we took the libretto of Rheingold went into the
Eng. Gardens, drove there a while, got out & went to the banks of the Isar
and read to each other. . . ." Ima does not say who accompanied her on
this occasion, nor does she record what she did on Tuesday, August 27.

Aug. 28, Munich
The "interesting men" have gone & in their places very interesting
ladies. Have dared to play on the piano here a little. Mrs. Cooper and
I carriaged to the Rheingold with little French lady. Had good seats

827-829—Whitehill the Wotan was an old friend of Mrs. Cooper's
with an interesting story to his career—and after the performance
met him. Quite a striking looking man. Has a good voice, too. . . .

Clarence Whitehill was an American baritone who had a distinguished
opera career on both sides of the Atlantic.[9] When Ima met him, he was
thirty-six years old. "Got home in time for dinner."

Aug. 29-Sept. 2, Munich

[Ima attended the opera again on Friday, August 30.] Glorious full
day! Burgstaller as Siegmund in the Valkyrie. Not anything could
have been arranged to delight me like that. Of course I've never
heard it sung so well before. . . . [Alois Burgstaller was a German
tenor who sang major Wagnerian roles in America and Europe.[10]]

Dreadful to come to earth and to find one's self out in the rain,
too, waiting for carriages. . . . The last Ring performance was a
brilliant scene. Many royal personages were discovered during
our walk in the garden. Crown princes of Romania, of Bavaria, &
some great French patron of art & music who was most hideously
gowned in bird head dress. . . . All were smoking & drinking quite
naturally! . . .

Met many delightful people at the Pension. Mrs. B [illegible]
of Brooklyn & the Woods also of Brooklyn. Mrs. Cooper, Miss
Cummings & I went to the Nat. Museum & rushed through, to our
regret.

The date of this National Museum excursion may have been Saturday,
August 31. Ima does not say what she did on Sunday, September 1, or
Monday, September 2. On September 3 Ima rejoined her tour companions in Innsbruck, Austria, and resumed her travel diary with no
mention of a decision she had just made. But in 1908 she wrote that "for
the last two months" of her 1907 tour (August and September) she had
known she would stay in Germany.

Sept. 3, Innsbruck

Here in the rain. Rode the train 2nd class with the cook in my
compartment of some Frau Gräfin who was herself 1st class. My

companion and I carried on an animated dialogue in German—
most enlightening! Great to find the crowd here—only the men
arrived the morning of Sept. 4—Wednesday. They were loaded
down with beautiful things from Russia and told the biggest fairy-
tales about the gold domes & 2 mil. dollar picture frame on a
picture painted by St. Luke! Made us feel everything we'd done was
poor in comparison. . . .

Sept. 5, Innsbruck

Pension Kayser. Mr. & Mrs. Thompson have had cables for Mr. T.
to go home immediately, so they are to go by Munich to Wiesbaden
tomorrow to the children. Mrs. T. may join us in Italy. . . .

Sept. 6, Zürich-Bellone

We went off in opposite directions—the rest of the party getting to
Zürich at 2:30. And in the flurry Miss Foster left her ticket in her
trunk & I my key. So Mr. F. came with the missing items to Lucerne,
where Mr. S. went to secure rooms. . . .

Sept. 7, Lucerne

Hotel L'Europe. 10:05 train arriving at 11:30 to the Lion designed
by Thorvaldsen in memory of the Swiss guards who defended the
Tuileries against the Jacobins in 1792. A most impressive piece of
work—out of solid rock in the mountain or cliff over a little pool of
water. Fascinating linen shops. In the morning at six-thirty went
to the Hofkirche [parish and monastery church] (for the organ
recital—fine instrument, fair playing. The "grand finale" being an
overrated imitation of storm in the Alps. The vox humana is very
good).

Sept. 8, Lucerne

By cog to Gütsch, or to a point from which we walked to Gütsch,—
through a woodsy place of great beauty.[11] The Alps are quite hidden
from view until afternoon & then foggy still. Came down by the
"shortest road in the world." In afternoon Miss Ione F. and I drove
to Wagner's home Tribschen but could not see in the house. Coming
home we had an experience with the driver—wanted us to get out at

the station so he could go to the races—we got out & paid what he
demanded!

Sept. 9, Lucerne

10:50 A.M. Boat-trip around Lake Lucerne! Cloudy & foggy as
usual. Got to Wm. Tell's chapel by 11:00. . . . Walked along the fine
road along the side of the lake to Flüelen. Longer & warmer in the
now bright sun than we imagined. Met many peddlers of cards
& some children who yodeled for us. Enjoyed this trip by foot &
decided to spend a summer in mountains.

Sept. 10, Interlaken

Metropole. Up & off at 9:00 A.M. Starting by boat from Lucerne
on the lake . . . by rail through Brünig Pass—a cog-wheel climb
through unsurpassed scenery. Then boat again to Giessbach where
we took a tiny cog road up to the hotel as the Giessbach Falls view
from up here most fine—would love to come back here for a quiet
sweet stay in country fascinating to roam in. By boat at 3:30 after
lunching—to Interlaken—getting a view of the Jungfrau for the first
time. . . .

Sept. 11, Grindelwald

Beautiful day—9 A.M. start by carriage towards lst sight of
Jungfrau then Mönch then Eiger then Matterhorn. . . . The marvel
of so much snow & ice when the day was so warm. Nothing in my
experience like it. Most pleasant trip back—rain at starting, but
cleared for a good sunset. . . . The impression of heavenly beauty
alone can be remembered & not written of.

Sept. 12, Montreux

9:05 start—all day trip to Montreux on Lake Geneva—going
through beautiful scenery & changing cars once . . . as we came
into sight of Lake Geneva—the dim & misty atmosphere over the
mountains, the bluish cast over the lake gave a Turneresque picture
to the scene from our high mountain road. . . . Palace Hotel the
scene of a lively fashionable crowd drinking & smoking women.

Sept. 13, Milan

L'Europe (fair). By Simplon Road through the Rhône valley with its old ruined castles—Château Valère at Sion—finally along Lake Maggiore after going through the long tunnel which wasn't so very uncomfortable—Immediate change of conditions on getting into Italy—warmer, unkempt lands, rundown looking houses—poverty. Trouble with tickets—got to hotel about 3 P.M. & went immediately to the Cathedral! . . . Got up early in Montreux to visit Chillon. Not awe inspiring from a distance but inside the bed of rock on which the prisoners spent their last night after coming out of the subterranean cell below—before execution, the gibbet where they were hung & conveniently thrown through the outside door in front of the execution spot—into the deep Lake Geneva below—the cell with wing in which the famous prisoner of Chillon, Bonivard, lived, & where Byron carved his own name.

Byron's 1816 poem "The Prisoner of Chillon" was inspired by his visit to the castle.

Sept. 14, Venice

Hotel Danieli. 7:30 A.M. start for Venice & met Mrs. Thompson on her way from Paris! Grand reunion. Comparatively poor country between Milan & V. but beautiful purple grapes and a view along a pretty lake. Venice 12:45. Into the gondolas & a very interesting trip up the Grand Canal to the Rialto Bridge where we went into a mysterious narrow passage—Tunnel under the Bridge of Sighs! . . . The Piazza at 5:30 P.M.! The glorified façade at this hour of St. Mark's was a most perfect moment. . . . Venice is far beyond my expectation. Nothing could be more enchanting.

Sept. 15, Venice

In afternoon spent a long time in St. Mark's—the Lady Chapel with St. Luke's miraculous painting of Madonna & Child on the altar. . . .

Sept. 16, Venice

Visited the inside of the Doge's Palace. . . . Went over the Bridge of Sighs—most gloomy. To Cathedral. . . . Ride down canal afternoon.

Browning home (died here), Wagner's house (died here) & 2nd
act of Tristan & Isolde. Byron's home. George Eliot lived in Hotel
Europa—in this hotel George Sand & Alfred de Musset. This
evening have been glancing over "Childe Harolde." My ideal of
Venice is a "city of the heart." . . .

Sept. 17, Venice
A morning of churches. . . . Saw lace & glass factory later. Morning
gondola ride on Canal with Mr. Scott.

Mr. Scott may have been saying his good-byes to Ima, since both knew
the tour was approaching its end. These two had enjoyed each other's
company for a summer—he, perhaps, more than she. "Musicians on the
water with their orchestra & single-lanterns & curious sight of boats all
paused to listen."

Sept. 18, Florence
All day trip. Pretty mountain scenery before arriving. Walked out
to Loggia after getting here, passing Ponte Vecchio. . . . This hotel
was once a Medici palace. . . .

Sept. 19, Florence
Went to Mrs. Orselli about miniatures early in morning. . . .
Decided to have two miniatures. She is a Texas girl married to an
Italian. Went from there to San Lorenzo stopping to buy gloves &
a skirt. Gloves @ £3.00 & very good ones. The door keeper at the
cloister on side of the Church bowed to me so I went in, thinking it
the entrance to the Medici tombs or something. Brought me a chair
to sit along the colonnade (?) & when I gave him a penny he brought
me three roses. . . . Finally discovered where I was, entered the
Church & into the Old Sacristy. . . .

Sept. 20, Florence
Everything closed in town. National Holiday. Cathedral open. . . .
Drive to San Miniato & magnificent view of Florence—river below
with reflection of crimson sky afterglow of the setting sun. . . .

Though Ima does not record this in her diary, on the evening before departing Florence for Naples, she happened to meet someone she knew: Alice McFarland, a wealthy young socialite from Houston, was also traveling that summer in Europe. Evidently Ima confided to Alice that she was hoping to stay in Germany, and Alice gave her the address of another Houston acquaintance, Leola Fisher, who was living in Berlin. Ima promptly wrote to Fisher and would receive an answer on October 4.

Sept. 21, Naples
Hard trip to Naples—trouble finding accommodations.

Sept. 22, Naples
Hotel des Etrangers. Shampoo—general clean up & washed my gray skirt!! Drive to San Martino through vile streets with sickening sights. Got Benedictine from original place & had good view of city with Vesuvius in the distance across bay. . . . Bay is grand & trip to Naples through rich valley country with beautiful vineyards.

Sept. 23, Naples
Shopping for corals. Few little Christmas presents.

[Sept. 24,] Capri, Sorrento
9:30 boat from Pier in front of hotel on the emerald green bay along rocky cliffs—in sight of Capri the high hill has the ruins of Villa Tiberius (?). After boat landing at Capri to Blue Grotto where the big boat anchored for us to take skiffs about 100 yds. from tiny opening of grotto. Stooped ourselves flat & slid into a cavern big enough to hold some 20 boats—and the sight quite took away my breath as satiated with lovely things as I am by now. The lighting is indescribable. . . . Lunch at Capri at Schweizerhof & there I went into the vineyard & cut purple grapes for lunch. . . . This Vittoria Hotel with lift from 160 feet below is magnificently situated. We are broken hearted to have so little time here—must come back. . . .

Sept. 25, Pompeii

Carriage from Vittoria Hotel through dusty dirty roads . . . to
Pompeii about 11 A.M. Stopped near electric roadway & took guide
at the gate (entrance 2:50)—guide 2:00 an hr. Museum entered
through old gateway & steps. Skeletons which were found filled with
soft plaster so they look very mummy like. Old water vessels, carved
pillars & things found in perfect preservation. . . . Hot day & too
tired to note much. . . . Now back to Naples by 2:30.

Sept. 26, Rome

<u>Eden Hotel</u>. Mr. Scott met us at depot & brought us to the nice
hotel. Rested (arrived about 2:15 P.M. & went out to view Forum
& then into Carcere Mamertino). . . . Walked to Colosseum
tremendous view, pausing to view Arch of Constantine, where
I think were only the St. Mark bronze horses. The grim old
Amphitheatre built in 80 A.D. . . . where were the bloody scenes of
slaughter of Christians & gladiatorial combat with lions. . . .

Sept. 27, Rome

To St. Peter's just to get impression. The Colonnade is most
impressive with its big round pillars. . . . Many colored marbles on
floor & walls. . . . Bronze statue of St. Peter is pagan-like—the right
foot kissed smooth—high altar & tomb of St. Peter. . . . First chapel
on right, Michelangelo Pieta—small slender limp figure of Christ. .
. . Into Vatican Sistine Chapel—ceiling paintings of Creation . . . all
by Michelangelo. . . . Swiss guards in many colored uniforms.

In the afternoon Via Appia—going past Temple of Vesta to Porta
Pauli by the side of which is the Protestant Cemetery with Keats &
Shelley & a large Pyramid. San Pauli . . . a magnificent church. . . .
Cross road going out to Via Appia . . . a fine view of Campagna &
Alban Hills & Aqueduct. Catacombs of Callixtus. Nice Franciscan
monk took us down to the deep cold dark passages. . . . Most bones
of martyrs have been taken away.

Sept. 28, Roma

Morning to Trajan Forum & column with bas relief of victory over
Dacians. . . . Over to Capital Museum . . . ! Carriage to Caracalla

Thermae. Remains of grandeur unsurpassed. . . . Afternoon by myself to Colosseum—walk up steps all around galleries—fine view of Rome—Over to Forum for a time there. . . .

Sept. 29, Rome

Borghese villa for sculpture and picture—only a short walk from hotel into the gardens. . . . Appian Way driving again as far out as the "Rotunda" noticing tombs with holes (for ashes) and cremation on a mound with big chimney—fine view. Horatio Apuleius & Seneca's tombs. Figures as of vestal virgins lying along roadside— Beautiful sky of blue.

Sept. 30, Rome

Size of St. Peter's gauged somewhat by noticing pen in St. Mark's hand! (high dome) which is 9 ft. long.—The dome itself size of rotunda in Pantheon. . . . Afternoon to churches. . . . Across to the Scala Santa supposed to be from Pontius Pilate's house up which Christ walked—brought to Rome by Empress Helena [in] 326— (in from Jerusalem really). Worshippers go up on knees. Before [them] on each side statues—one on right Christ being kissed by Judas.—Tea on Corso—lovely.

Oct. 1, Rome

Mr. Scott left us for Heidelberg. . . . [This was not the last Ima would see of Charles Scott. He would visit her in Berlin. Meanwhile, she continued her sightseeing in Rome.] St. Peter's first—then Sistine Chapel—Taking first the ceiling again by Michelangelo then the frescoes on walls. . . . Opera at night Il Duchino by Lecocq.

Oct. 2, Rome

Sick in morning—packing. Afternoon shopping.

Oct. 3, Florence

Through Pisa to Florence. Drove between rains to Cathedral [dating from] 1060. Through old bronze doors to interior. . . . Very lovely. Into Florence tired and in the rain—to this Pension Quisisana.

Oct. 4, Florence

**Raining in morning—Letter from Leola Fisher about my stay in
Berlin this winter. Uffizi this afternoon till four.**

Here Ima's 1907 diary ends rather abruptly. October 4 was the last day
recorded and the first mention of her decision to remain in Germany.
Ima had known Leola Fisher for several years, and the two had attended
many of the same parties and dances in Houston. In the summer of
1907 they may have discussed their travel plans before Ima left in June.
Leola was sailing to Europe in July for an extended stay. According to a
Houston Post article dated July 7, 1907, "Mr. and Mrs. H. F. Fisher and
family" sailed on the *Kronprinz Wilhelm* on July 16. Leola's parents
"and family" probably included Leola's maternal grandmother, Selma
Voight (who then called herself Mrs. White), as well as Leola and her
eighteen-year-old brother, Henry. Leola was to stay abroad "indefinitely,
principally for pleasure and sightseeing, incidentally, however, some
attention will be given to voice culture. Mr. Fisher, who remains abroad
with his sister, will devote earnest and assiduous study to the higher
cultivation of his remarkable talent for the violin." Ima's Berlin diary
does not mention Leola's pursuit of "voice culture" or any other musical
studies. Henry (Buddy) and his violin are part of the diary, but if he took
lessons, they are not mentioned. Leola's letter to Ima was a response to
Ima's September query about staying in Berlin. Leola's and Ima's letters
to each other have not been found.

There is a mystery at the end of Ima Hogg's 1907 diary: On the last two
pages, not in Ima's handwriting, is a list of German words and phrases,
mostly musical terms. Whose handwriting was this? Ima did not begin
her German lessons or her music studies until 1908. The two pages are
reproduced here with translations. Ima's translations are in italics, but
she translated only a handful of words.

Die Künste	*The Notes*
Die Musik	*music*
musikalisch	*musical*
ein Musiker	*musician*

sind Sie musikalisch	*are you musical*
wir wollen etwas musizieren	*we wish some music*
	(we would like to make
	some music [together])
ich lernte nur für den	I learned to play music
Hausbedarf Musik	only for use at home
Musikalien	*pieces of music* (sheet music,
	musical compositions, etc.)
Instrumentenhändler	musical instrument dealer
die Note	the musical note
~~Noten?~~ Notenpapier	sheet music paper, staff
	paper
ein Notenbuch	a sheet music book
die Notenlinie	the staff (line)
auf der untersten Linie	on the lowermost staff line
zwischen der ersten und ???	between the first and second
zweiten Linie	line
die Doppelnote	the double note
die ganze Note	the whole note
[next page]	
die Halbnote	the half note
die Viertelnote	the quarter note
die Achtelnote	the eighth note
die ??? Sechzehntelnote	the sixteenth note
das ??? Zweiunddreißigstel	the thirty-second
das Vierundsechzigstel	the sixty-fourth
der Punkt	the point (e.g., after a note)
drei Achtel	three eighths
Kirchenmusik	church music
das Singen	the singing
singen	(to) sing
ein Gesang	a song, such as an aria
	or chant

der [illegible]	
die Noten	the musical notes
Melodie	melody
Singen Sie bitte ein Lied	Please sing a song
der [illegible]	(for me, us)
eines Liedes	of a song

On the two pages following are two pencil sketches, unidentified, undated. One is a young man's head in profile, most likely drawn by Ima, who was quite talented as an artist. On the facing page is a crude drawing of a young woman seated on a bench, holding a walking stick. This sketch appears to have been done by a different hand—one somewhat lacking artistic talent. On this same page, behind the sketch of the young woman, is the faint outline of another drawing evidently begun by the person who drew the young man's head. It is an unfinished sketch of the same young man's face, but only his nose, mouth, and chin, as though the artist had abandoned that sketch for the completed one opposite. Who was the handsome young man? Did he draw the sketch of Ima? Ima Hogg was good at keeping secrets.

On October 9, 1907, Ima bade farewell to her travel companions in Florence and boarded a train that would take her to Berlin the next day. There she was met by Leola Fisher and Leola's brother Henry and went with them to stay at Leola's grandmother's residence. That was October 10. Ima immediately began a whirl of concertgoing in music-rich Berlin: From October 12 to December 16 she attended a total of sixteen musical events, either operas or concerts, an average of two a week for eight weeks.[12] In the midst of this crowded musical calendar, Ima moved with Leola, Henry, and their grandmother to an apartment in the affluent suburb of Charlottenburg.

Ima recorded some, but not all, of the details when she began a new diary on New Year's Day, 1908.

Figure 3. Sketch of unknown young man, 1907

Figure 4. Sketch of Ima Hogg, 1907

2

The Charlottenburg Diary

This diary is a small leather-bound *Tagebuch* with a brass lock and, presumably, a key.[1] Ima Hogg wrote faithfully in it almost every day from January 1 to February 29, 1908. Here the diary breaks off with no explanation, and many blank pages are left in the little book. What made Ima stop writing in it? She did not record what she did for nearly eight months. She returned to Houston in October 1908.

This diary, like Ima's 1907 travel journal, has some secrets, the most obvious and curious being the nicknames she gave to Leola and Henry Fisher and their grandmother (Mrs. Selma White), all of whom shared the apartment with her. Ima also bestowed nicknames on Siegfried Goetze (Leola's "swain," who would marry Leola in 1910) and Charles Scott, a 1907 tour companion who came to visit Ima. Ima did not divulge their real names, but toward the end of her diary she sometimes—perhaps forgetfully—referred to "Leola." Ima evidently wished to keep her diary private, under lock and key.

Using nicknames instead of real names may have made her feel secure, but anyone living in that Berlin apartment would have known immediately to whom the nicknames referred. For convenience's sake, here is a list of proper names and nicknames Ima gave some of them in the 1908 diary:

Figure 5. 1908 diary

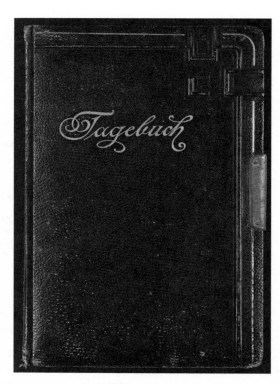

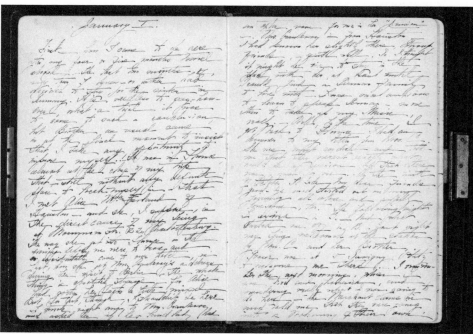

Figure 6. 1908 diary, first page

List of Persons

Charles Scott, Ima's travel companion in 1907 ("Areal")

Edna Peterson, Ima's friend, an American studying music
   in Berlin

Fräulein Liese, Ima's German teacher

G. Goetze, father of Siegfried and Gerhard, architect, resident
   owner of the building at Mommsenstrasse 22, where the Fishers
   rented an apartment[2]

Gerhard Goetze, younger brother of Siegfried Goetze

Helena Lewyn, Ima's friend, an American studying music
   in Berlin

Henry Fisher ("Buddy," "Hiawatha")

Leola Fisher ("Mrs. Cranberry," "Mrs. C." "Merchant,"
   "Madam," "the Sphinx")

Martin Krause, Ima's music teacher

Selma White, Leola Fisher's sixty-eight-year-old grandmother
   ("Grosse")

Siegfried Goetze, Leola Fisher's beau ("Wälsung")

Xaver Scharwenka, Ima's music teacher

On the first page of the diary, Ima wrote:

Berlin Germany
<u>1908</u>
Mommsenstr. 22
Charlottenburg

Jan. 1

First, how I came to be here after my four or five months travel
abroad. The last two months of my tour, I knew or rather had
decided to stay for the winter in Germany. It is needless to say,
however, what a trial it was to come to such a conclusion. But
Brother [Will Hogg] as usual came in at the final moment to insist

that I take any opportunity to improve myself! It was in Florence almost at the close of my trip—still without any definite places to locate myself in—that I met Alice McFarland of Houston—and she, I suppose, is the direct cause of my being at Mommsenstr. 22, Charlottenburg.[3] The way she got into Florence on the evening before we were to leave and so accidentally came to our hotel, in fact, how she got Mrs. Cranberry's address during her visit to Berlin, the whole thing is absolutely strange for Alice had gotten her facts a little mixed. But for that, though, I shouldn't be here. I wrote right away to Mrs. Cranberry and asked her if her landlady had an extra room for me in her "Pension." Mrs. Cranberry is from Houston. I had known her slightly there through friends—quite well. [Perhaps Ima meant that she herself had a slight acquaintance with Leola Fisher and knew the rest through hearsay.] So I thought it might be nice to stay in the place with her, at least until I could find a German family to live with—I was most anxious to learn to speak German—more than to take up my music, really.—Well, by the time I got back to Florence, I had an answer to my letter from Mrs. C. She was most cordial and told me that they weren't in exactly what would be a Pension, but that there was a room for me.

On the ninth of October, I bade my dear friends good-bye and started out on my journey all alone and awfully lonesome, too. The following night I arrived in B [Berlin]. And what started me off in B just right was being welcomed at the station by Mrs. C. and her Brother [Henry Fisher]. Grosse [Ima may have given Leola's grandmother the name "Grosse," mistakenly thinking that "Grosse" is short for Grossmutter] was at 5 Savigny Platz to welcome me there. [Savignyplatz was a small square with residences surrounding a garden. Evidently Leola's grandmother and the Fishers were living there but were about to move to an apartment at Mommsenstrasse 22, a few blocks away.]

I remember the next morning when I was tired and homesick and wondering really what I was going to do here. The Merchant came in and told me that they were going into a Wohnung [apartment] of their own. Then I felt hopeless. The next moment though she told me that they had a little room vacant, perhaps too small, but that if I found it suitable, I might come and live with her

Figure 7. Mommsenstrass 22, Charlottenburg, 2018.

and her family. Imagine such kindness. So the first of November,
after a time of Möbel [furniture] hunting, we stepped into the
snuggest sweetest little Wohnung in the world, all fixed up by
the Cranberry Merchant [Leola] and myself. I got a Bechstein to
practice on and began lessons with Xaver Scharwenka at his home.
[Scharwenka was a fifty-eight-year-old German pianist, composer,
and teacher of music, a founder of the Klindworth-Scharwenka
Conservatory in Berlin.[4] He accepted Ima Hogg as a private pupil.]
If you had been told the size of my room and what I wanted to
have in it, you'd never believe it possible to put half of it there. All
my furniture is <u>white</u>—a tiny bed, everything had to be tiny and
made to order—oh! "Gebrüder"[5]—a shrank [Schrank, wardrobe],
a washtisch [Waschtisch, vanity], a Tisch [table)], and the Klavier
[piano], not to mention the two chairs. The walls of the little den
give a nice rosy pink effect, so at the windows I have a sweet little
mull curtain and forehangings [Ima's translation of Vorhänge,
the German word for drapes] of dark green, the lovely little rug to
match. Very cheerful looking, and I love to be in it.

Ima had settled happily in Charlottenburg, then an independent city
with a population of two hundred thousand just west of Berlin. It was
an affluent neighborhood, home to many artists, musicians, and writers.
Her Mommsenstrasse 22 address was a multistory building with eight
apartments. The owner, who lived there and rented to others, was listed
in the City Directory of 1908 as G. Goetze, an architect. He lived there
with his family, among them his sons: Siegfried, who would marry Leola
Fisher in 1910, and Gerhard, "the little Goetze boy." Other renters included Felix Hollaender, a noted playwright and critic, who later worked
with Max Reinhardt, the famous stage director, at the Deutsches Theater,
and whose brother, Victor, and nephew, Friedrich, were musicians and
composers. By the time Ima had moved to Mommsenstrasse 22, the Jewish population of Charlottenburg numbered approximately twenty-two
thousand.[6] Today, evidence of the large Jewish presence in Charlottenburg can be found in the great number of the so-called *Stolpersteine* (lit.
stumbling stones), brass plaques commemorating the victims of National
Socialism and installed by the artist Gunter Demnig in the pavement in

front of their last address. In Charlottenburg-Wilmersdorf alone there are more than 3,450 stones. Oddly enough, Ima does not mention any of the residents of Mommsenstrasse 22 except the Goetzes, though surely she must have known of them. The Fishers may have rented an apartment facing the courtyard at the back of the house. Some houses in this area had a "garden house," which, like all apartments in the building, were accessible only through the front gate. Ima once mentions coming home from the opera and having to climb over the fence "to ring the bell" because she had no key to the front gate.

"There's lots to remember before this New Year but I've spent too much time already." Indeed there was "lots to remember." From October 12, two days after her arrival in Berlin, to December 16, 1907, Ima went with Leola, or Leola and Henry, to an opera or a concert two or three nights a week, for a total of sixteen events. She did not record these in her diary, but she kept the programs, sometimes making comments about the performances and noting "Leola" or "Leola & Henry" on the program cover. On three occasions Ima, always independent, may have attended events by herself.[7] Evidently Ima wrote to her family during this time, although her letters, if they survived, have not been located. On December 30, Ima's youngest brother, Tom, then in the US Marines, wrote to her at the Mommsenstrasse 22 address, thanking her for her letters and for the pipes she had sent him for Christmas.[8] Ima did not say how she spent Christmas, but she celebrated New Year's Eve at Mommsenstrasse 22.

> Of course, we sat up with the old year—poor old year—and watched this one come in, and yelled "Prosit Neujahr" [Cheers to the New Year]—rather Buddy did—like everybody else.
> Then we all wished each other happiness and kissed all around.
> Melted "Blei" [lead] and they turned into the cold water in no shapes at all, just a muddle.

In some parts of Germany it is customary on New Year's Eve to melt lead in a spoon over a flame and pour it into cold water, where it congeals into shapes from which you can tell the future. A ball means luck will be rolling in. A cross means someone will die, and so on.

We have been dreadful about getting up and going to bed, too—so
among our resolutions—one was to rise at half past seven. After
staying up till half after one that was hard. But out of the darkness
came the faint squeak of Buddy's violin—oh so faithful. It was
nearly light and I hopped out of bed and was dressed in time to do
a few studies on the piano before breakfast. The sun was out in all
the brightness it is able to assume in such a friendless country. The
Madam and I went for a long walk. I hadn't been practicing long
after my return before who should appear but Areal.[9] Immediately
after him, the Madam's young swain from across the way—the
Wälsung, appeared, too. [The "young swain" was Siegfried Goetze,
son of the building's landlord, Gerhard Goetze. Ima, with her
knowledge of Wagnerian opera, dubbed him "Wälsung" after
Siegfried, the son of the Wälsung family of the Ring Cycle.] They
stayed until late in the afternoon and we all drank egg-nog together.
And at night, we actually went to bed early—half past nine, we
watched the clock.

Jan. 2

Practice before Frühstück [breakfast] again—but Frühstück was
late! Fräulein Liese, my deutsche Lehrerin [German teacher] came
at half past ten and I began my lessons again. During my Stunde
[hour-long lesson], Areal rang up to ask Mrs. Cranberry and me to
go to [the] opera that night. Edna Peterson came in, had lunch with
us and played a Chopin Ballad and a Meditation by Tchaikovsky.
She plays very well indeed, is quite young, studies with Mr. Spanuth
until her real teacher Mr. Rudolph Ganz returns.

August Spanuth, pupil of Rudolph Ganz, was a German composer,
pianist, and teacher; Rudolph Ganz, Swiss-born, was an internationally
known composer, musician, and teacher.[10] Edna Peterson was one
of many young Americans studying music in Berlin. She was one of
twelve students boarding with a family in the Charlottenburg area
near Ima.[11]

At the opera I wore my white cloth suit [Ima was still in mourning
for her father and was not yet wearing bright colors.], Mrs. C. her

fawn suit with the lovely yellow waist—we had grand seats near the
king's box in the first tier. I Pagliacci with Kraus and Hoffmann
was given first.[12] The Barber of Bagdad—Knüpfer as the Barber,
Sommer, tenor, Hempel, soprano—gave an excellent performance—
Strauss directed![13] Decidedly the only noteworthy production I've
been to in Berlin. Bitterly cold coming home.—But I must mention
Kraus again. In Munich, I heard him as Tristan and Siegfried—the
latter in good voice. But in Pagliacci I didn't recognize him—his
voice was lyrical almost and so beautiful.

Jan. 3

And yesterday—I forgot to say—Mrs. C. and I visited the Dresdner
Bank—me to cash 500 marks Brother had sent me. Then the Madam
was all excitement to get to Wertheim's [a department store] to meet
the Wälsung. She left me in great haste and I went off in search of
ribbon and a coat hanger to cover for Hiawatha.

   I sat up after I came home from the opera and made a real
pretty little birthday gift for his blue room. So today—the
third—he was presented with it and some nice things from the
Cranberry Merchant which the Wälsung had helped her select.
The police visited me again, for the fifth time, about my passport
and left sassy orders about it. So when Areal appeared again in
the afternoon, I told him my troubles and he promised to save
me the trouble of going to the American Embassy. The Wälsung
again and his Brother came in for Buddy's birthday cake and
egg-nog. That night, Grosse, Mrs. C., Hiawatha and I went in an
auto—as usual—to Mozart Saal [Mozart Hall] to hear Busoni
with the Philharmonic Orchestra.[14] Sauret played Busoni's violin
concerto—which I think is absolutely without interest, and Felix
Senius, a good tenor, gave Liszt's sonnets from Petrarch with Liszt's
orchestral accompaniment, then Busoni's piano.[15] An interesting
and lovely tone poem was a Bacchanal by [space left blank], the
first performance, and the composer came out—a white-headed
man—and loved his delighted acknowledgment of the applause. In
the audience, I noticed Lhévinne. [Josef Lhévinne was a Russian
concert pianist.[16]] He must be spending his winter here as I noticed
him at a Godowsky recital some weeks before.[17] Grosse slept

through most of the numbers. After coming home, of course we had
the usual soirée and got to bed late.

Jan. 4

Dutch [Ima's slang for "Deutsch" or German] lesson. My breakfast
food arrived [brought by a servant] and [the servant] stayed a moment to hand me my passport—oh! joy and relief. In the afternoon,
Areal came and spent the time making himself miserable again—I
hoped he had understood after what I told him last summer. I acted
like a cold-blooded vampire, he told me I was heartless—but when I
seemed to be sympathizing with him, it didn't do, alas! Well, I was
upset anyhow. He's off for Heidelberg in the morning.

Ima Hogg had disposed of yet another ardent suitor. She and Charles
Scott had had a romantic summer, rowing on Lake Windermere, reading
Ruskin, fishing, taking a gondola in Venice, all to no avail.

Jan. 5

Got up late—permissible on Sunday—and made a wild dash for the
Königliche Opernhaus [Royal Opera House]—the box office closes
at one and by that time all the tickets are gone for the week. We got
good seats for the Walküre and Siegfried.—Edna Peterson and Miss
Palmer [another American studying music in Berlin] came in for tea.

Jan. 6

Fine German lesson. I certainly am going to see if I can't get
something into my head. The usual routine. Went to the library—
I got some Mark Twain sketches and bought a Dutch [German]
grammar, atlas. I studied my Walküre some, too, and bought the
score of Siegfried. The evening we spent in much enthusiasm over
our diaries.

Jan. 7

Practiced badly. Went to the Kaufhaus [department store] and
invested in silk for a kimono, lavender for myself and pale blue for
L. [Leola] and lace and a pattern.

Jan. 8

After all our efforts to start the days out right—Theresa, the Dienstmädchen [maid], herself gets up too late—and has all the meals most irregularly. Neither Leola [Beginning here, Ima occasionally mentions Leola Fisher by her given name.] nor Grosse would take it upon themselves to mention the desirability of a change, so Buddy braced up like a little man and went into the kitchen all alone, and must have talked all right, for Frühstück [breakfast] came at half past eight, dinner at half past one, and tea at half past six—just as they always should. I read the chapter—after breakfast—in the "Imitation of Christ" by Thomas à Kempis— which has gotten to be a habit that not exactly suits the family but which they endure like angels. Then Buddy beat me mercilessly at two games of checkers.—Practice Gnomenreigen [Dance of the Gnomes], Liszt Etudes by Chopin and some technic.

My first lesson since the holidays came this afternoon at 3:30. Xaver was etwas erkältet [had a slight cold] but was quite nice at the lesson. The Gnomenreigen he told me to play some slower than I've been studying it, and gave me an etude by himself. Staccato op. 27.—Rode on Untergrund [subway] as far as Zoologischer Garten—stopped on my way to the music store and bought some sweet-smelling yellow flowers. A man said something to me, scared the life out of me. Then another just before turned from Kant [Kantstrasse]. I thought [he] was going to insist on walking with me. I really was never more frightened. They say Berlin is a terrible place for such things—my first and I hope my last experience.

Came back to find a pretty little desk lamp on the table. I am writing by it now.—

As usual when going to Mozart Saal an electric Droschke [cab] was the means of getting there tonight. Bronisław Huberman, a violinist, was the soloist—Spohr concerto & Tchaikovsky concerto with orchestra—the latter with excellent spirit.[18] He has much ability but some noticeable faults. The audience, however, seemed to overlook anything of an unpleasant nature and was wildly enthusiastic. A new piano and violin piece by W. Junker from the manuscript—quite lovely, nothing unusual. Richard Singer—

Mitwirkung [accompaniment] played Liszt's piano concerto with orchestra. Came home in Bedag [electric taxicab]![19]

Jan. 9

Fräulein [Ima's German teacher, Miss Liese] didn't come for my lesson. A horrid day, raining, but tonight it turned into a snow storm and we had to take a Bedag to the Königliche Opernhaus [Royal Opera House]. "Die Walküre" began at seven o'clock and we listened to a very good performance. Kraus was a very good Siegmund, Hiedler a good Sieglinde if she hasn't a very good voice. Fräulein Kurt of Braunschweig was the guest and took the part of Brünnhilde most gracefully and with a beautiful voice.[20] I wonder that the Kaiser would stand for such poor scenery as they use here, and the stage management for the Wagnerian opera is really dreadful. Strauss conducted. Came home in a Bedag.

Jan. 10

Woke up with the headache, so decided to have a good rest rather than do anything else, as a consequence didn't get up until about one o'clock. Snow was heavy over everything, and Mrs. C. reported a glorious sunny cold day. And at her suggestion, we went for a sleigh ride about half after two. That is—Grosse, Mrs. C. and I went, Buddy absolutely refused to budge. I can't think any of us had ever been sleighing and the novelty was intoxicating, the cold, cold air in the face, the nice warm rugs tucked around you, soft furs to snuggle up in and the merry people in the streets. But we were soon on the country road out in the Grünewald! It's long getting there, though. We went by way of Bismarck Allee which is lined with really beautiful residences, some of which have large gardens. One I remember had terraces, four or five facing the river, and I can imagine how sweet it must be in the summer. Nothing, I'm sure, could have made a lovelier scene, however, than the snow today. We hadn't those picturesque little Tannenbaums [fir trees] at home in our garden, and our snow scenes for that one reason if no other could not be so fascinating. The dear dumpy little trees were absolutely impudent-looking so dressed up with soft white snow.

On the high road, a photographer had placed himself to humor a few foolish people, and we were so charmed with ourselves and everything else in general that we consented to pay eight marks for three pictures of ourselves. I know I for one really looked a fright—a pinched purple expression is [not] very likely to turn out well—but I wouldn't take anything for the big long-haired horses, our fat Dutchy Kutscher [coachman] in his bear-like looking apparel, to say nothing of the three of us in the snowy woods. We went as far as "Onkel Toms Hütte" [Uncle Tom's Cabin]—fancy such a place in Germany![21] I suppose from the looks of the place they knew just that much too about the meaning of it. At the "Hütte," we had some port wine, and then started for home. We met any number of good-looking sleighs and the people in them evidently were enjoying themselves as much as we for they all smiled cheerfully at us as though we were old friends. And the woods, too, were full of people walking, laughing and behaving like children at a picnic. No people like these Germans for spontaneous enjoyment of every phase of life. They wouldn't miss a frolic on a day like this for anything.

Jan. 11

Practiced only a half hour today! Suppose I am wicked but the truth is I simply didn't feel like doing anything. Went to Pracht's for a hair-dressing preparatory to going to a tea at Mrs. Ganz's. [Mary Ganz was the American wife of the musician Rudolph Ganz. She gave voice lessons and evidently befriended many students.]

As usual, we were late there, not getting there until six o'clock, so we had very little time to stay before time to rush for [the] opera at seven. Lots of nice-looking people were there. Sauret and his daughter, Mrs. Spanuth whom we met and among several others, Arthur Hartmann, the violinist.

Emile Sauret, a French violinist, was a well-known concert artist. Mrs. Spanuth was the wife of composer August Spanuth. Arthur Hartmann was an American-born violinist, a year older than Ima. He sent her a photograph/postcard of himself: "To Miss Hogg—Cordially Arthur Hartmann, Berlin 1908."[22]

The ladies were taking their times about being flirted with by
him, and Leola and I decided we didn't "choose" anything of the
kind. Had a few words with Mrs. Brooks, Miss Palmer and Edna
Peterson. Missed the overture to Siegfried! The performance was
excellent. The whole cast was fine, good actors with beautiful voices.
Had heard Kraus as Siegfried in Munich and his role was equally
well taken tonight. Mustn't forget to mention the exciting fight
with the dragon, he was the most life-like old fellow and the fiercest
I ever saw. Fräulein Kurt who was guest in the Walküre the other
night was Brünnhilde again tonight. The voice was really one of
the grandest I ever heard, so fresh and full and clear. If only Kraus
wouldn't howl so at the lovely part in the last act. We came home in
a Bedag as usual, I for one much under the spell of the music—as I
am now. We had our "tea"—or chocolate after we got home.

Jan. 12

Slept as late as I wanted to—and for breakfast had dinner. Read a
little bit, played a little bit—and felt altogether like doing nothing.
Wälsung's brother, the little Goetze boy, came over and played
all the games he knew with us. Then Leola made him say English
things and laughed herself sick.

Jan. 13

Fräulein is ill, I suppose, didn't come this morning. And I haven't
felt a bit like doing anything.—It is time to start if I'm going to have
any sort of a lesson on Tuesday. Studied my German a little though,
and read a Life of Chopin—a short one by Ernest J. Oldmeadow.
This afternoon, I cut out a pale blue batiste chemise for Leola and
she has been sewing it up and putting the lace on the neckline. She
has just come in, cheeks in a flush, all excitement over, I imagine,
her first garment. I wonder how much will be finished. [Evidently
Leola was not much given to sewing.] Played Buddy some games
of checkers. I beat one game, tied another, but I don't feel a bit
triumphant because I know I was simply "let beat." Then the young
man proceeded to tell me about some of his young love affairs, too
funny for words.

Jan. 14

I am absolutely no-account, good-for-nothing, and if I don't
bestir myself, I shall never get anything into my head. Really, I
feel hopeless, have been so for days, and now I think if I say so I
shall perhaps be able to shake off a real weariness of spirits. I am
homesick and stupid and lonesome and utterly miserable.

I did practice more today—and didn't learn much either.
Something is wrong. I got out for a little walk today, the first since
Thursday. Mrs. Cranberry and I went to the library in Kantstrasse
and back by Kurfürstendamm.

Jan. 15

Practiced pretty well—had to for my lesson. Xaver is not at all well,
but he was an old dear at the lesson. My lesson was better than I
thought it would be. I like the way he showed me to play staccato in
his etude. In a very naïve way he told me that when he was young,
and played in concert, that etude was very popular, in Petersburg he
was encored three times. I told him I thought it very pretty indeed,
and he was as pleased as a child—imagine—and ran off to bring his
new concerto to show me. It certainly looked difficult—he says Risler
will most likely play it the first time. I've never taken any of my time
talking before but today I asked Mr. S. questions about a few things,
and he is too clever and funny for words. He said Marteau's being
placed at the head of the Hofschule [Hochschule] would be a death
blow to the Joachim school. And he said he felt so sorry for Halir
who by succession should fall to the place at the head of the school.[23]
From my lesson went to Wertheim's to meet Leola so we could get
tickets for some concerts. We got some for the Walzertraum for
tonight. Have just returned and have had the usual feast afterwards.
Walzertraum has beautiful scenery and costumes—is horrid and
inexcusably so—I do not think it would be tolerated in America.
Theater des Westens [a Berlin opera house] was most gorgeous. Had
been feeling fine today—I think the blues are out of my system for
a while anyhow. Had several letters, too, those "old sweethearts of
mine"—with the same sad tale! Well. [These letters, like many letters
that came to Ima, have not been located.]

Jan. 16

Woke up with a headache but took something for it before
breakfast—which by the way was at half past eleven. Practiced
on Kreisleriana by Schumann. Scharwenka told me I could take
my choice of that or a Chopin Ballade or Faschingsschwank [aus
Wien, "Carnival Prank from Vienna," one of eight short pieces
that constitute Schumann's Kreisleriana]. I may begin by taking
up the Chopin. Went to Mark Hamburg's recital at Beethoven
Saal [Beethoven Hall] the greatest combination of virtue and
faultlessness I ever saw.[24] The programme was stupendous. I
think it is a case of too much temperament. He really plays faster
than you can think—he may have played some of the Etudes by
Chopin, clearly I don't know—for I couldn't keep up with him.
Mrs. Cranberry and I went in an auto and came back by car—It was
raining. Just like us—was a beautiful night when we went there.
Noticed Lhévinne in the audience again—good many distinguished
people were in the audience. Abell and two or three critics sat in the
same row with us.[25]

Jan. 17

We sat up so late at home last night after the concert that I felt like
a boiled owl this morning—headache all day. But I went to practice
and got in some good work. Such a horrid day that I didn't go out.
Tonight Buddy and I played checkers and I beat [the] first game—he
had the second. Then he began telling me about birds and reptiles—
most interestingly—and I find myself up later than I intended
again. We are dreadful about ever going to bed—as naughty as if
we'd never made any resolutions about ten o'clock at night and eight
for rising.

Jan. 18

Practiced about three hours—some of it in earnest and some
in "play." Went to Pracht's for a shampoo. Fräulein is still sick.
Tonight Buddy and I played Saint-Saëns, Rode concertos and
Vieuxtemps' Fantasie and the Chopin Valse in D-flat. How lovely
to sit at the beautiful grand piano in the sweet little Wohnzimmer

[living room]—and now it's ten o'clock. We have a new leather chair which is now residing with great dignity in the bay window.

Jan. 19

Went to bed late—got up late this morning, but had Frühstück in time to rush downtown for tickets to Tristan and Isolde at the Königliche Opernhaus [Royal Opera House] before the box office closed. We stood on Unter den Linden [one of Berlin's most famous boulevards] for some time because we saw the streets lined with waiting people—so imagined maybe the Kaiser was coming. All the excitement turned out to be over a paltry company of soldiers due to march down the street behind a brass band. Goetze Junge came over—took tea and related all sorts of excitement about Berlin highwaymen.[26] And told us too that troublesome times are ahead for the government. The "Arbeitsleute" [working-class people] are quite dissatisfied and he says the crown prince will never be a Kaiser—a revolution very likely, I suppose to occur at the Kaiser's death.

Jan. 20

Fräulein appeared this morning—and she looked as if she really had been sick. I think she had been studying too much, preparing for the university where she wants to study Theology! Whatever she intends to do with a course of that in a college! She stayed two hours, and we had a beautiful time talking about the "country"— music, etc. I told her my troubles—all about my piano having become a perfect wreck and wanting to change my piano teacher, too. Xaver is a dear, and may be all right, but I really don't think he is deep enough in his teaching—and not careful enough. He tells me such outrageous things about myself, too, that it makes me mistrust him. Well, after Fräulein left, I was worn out—with thinking in German so hard for so long at a stretch. After lunch I practiced two hours, too—though I was tired. We went to tea.

Edouard Risler is at the Philharmonie Saal [Philharmonic Hall]. His playing is pleasing—in taste I suppose—it is not always according to mine, however. Came and went in a Bedag. Last night,

Leola and I had a good long talk about my playing.—I have been
quite sick about it for some time, and one day asked L. for her idea
as to what is wrong with it. A dozen things are—at heart—but the
greatest thing she thinks is lack of cleanness in my fast runs! I know
that something has gotten radically wrong with my fingers. I may
not pick them up quickly enough. I have not decided. An average
practice though of two hours a day at my stage in technic will never
do—and I must manage to get in three and a half or four hours.

Jan. 21

The usual day—late rising—only about two hours practice. This
afternoon got out for a brisk walk and shopped a while in the
Nachbarschaft [neighborhood]. Tonight wrote some letters I've been
promising myself to write—for ages—to Brother, Bess, Mrs. Graves,
and a card to Mrs. Leach and to Mrs. Ben Thompson. [Mrs. Ben
(Lucy) Thompson was one of Ima's travel companions on the 1907
tour.]

Jan. 22

Lesson today—played first fourteen pages of Kreisleriana. Xaver is
always feeling badly but was all right and I had a fair lesson. Went
to the Kaufhaus [department store] after my lesson to meet Leola
and we did a little shopping there—came home in Bedag. Were to
have gone to a concert tonight—Hamburg again—but for some
reason it was called off.

Jan. 23

Fräulein didn't come. Practiced and took a little walk. Went to an
Elite concert at Grosse Philharmonie Saal [Great Philharmonic
Hall]—Busoni and [space left blank] were the artists most
interesting to me. After Busoni's second number—Don Juan
Fantasie and the encore, Chopin's "Raindrops" Prelude—we left.
Busoni's technic is excellent and he plays with great intelligence
and taste. However, in the Prelude, he utterly failed to bring out the
sweet melody with any feeling whatsoever. We came home by the
U-Bahn [subway] for a wonder though we lived up to our record by
going to the concert in a Bedag.

Jan. 24

Were up until after one o'clock after the concert and got up late. This morning, Fräulein came to Leola and said that the king was going to [illegible word crossed out] be at the opera Monday night on his birthday, so Mrs. Cranberry and I went down to the "Königliche" [Royal Opera House] in the customary haste. Droschke [taxicab] at the Bahnhof [train station] and all only to find that it was an invitation affair. Mrs. Cranberry's birthday is on the 27th also and we were anxious to celebrate. Got home in time for lunch. Grosse and Leola and Buddy all went to Arthur Hartmann's for coffee this afternoon—I started to practicing but got too sleepy, had to have a nap.

Heard Eugène Ysaÿe at the Philharmonie—Bach G-dur [G major] concerto, . . . Moor Concerto in G and the Beethoven D-dur [D major] concerto. The audience went mad over him and we along with the rest. After playing two pieces—Romance by Svendsen and Ballade Polonaise by Wieniawski, he was recalled to thunderous applause at least a dozen times, only responding with appreciative bows.[27] His tone is to me the very wonderful thing of all the lovely things in his playing—a very weak way of expressing a little bit of what I really feel. We saw Lhévinne and his wife—Sauret and his daughter and Arthur Hartmann in the audience. So many familiar faces one finds after going so often. We had great fun picking out the most conspicuous freaks [referring to people who are passionately or obsessively interested in one subject].

Jan. 25

We sat up until three o'clock just talking—and, of course, all got up late. Had my German lesson and practiced more than usual during the day. Went to Tristan and Isolde tonight. It began at seven o'clock, and though we rushed there in an auto, had to stand outside while the overture was being played. Why I enjoyed Tristan so much I cannot say—unless it is because L. adores this music regardless of the opera being so poorly performed. The cast was dreadful— Plaichinger as Isolde failed on account of not enough dramatic ability—Grüning's voice is terrible for anything. His Tristan was bad and Bragäne sung by Frau Goetze [no relation to the Goetze family at Mommsenstrasse 22] was as bad as possible. Bachmann, however, was an excellent Kurwenal, and an American, Griswold, sang König Marke beautifully—Strauss conducted.[28] As usual, the staging was poor, a farce, and it is shocking to think that in Berlin, a musical center, it is tolerated. Came home in Bedag.

Jan. 26

Mademoiselle Cruelle—the Merchant's French teacher—took dinner with us. Had music in the afternoon and egg-nog. Mlle. stayed for tea and later Herr Keller came. He is a friend of a friend of Leola's. He has a beautiful tenor voice and is studying for Wagner opera. We played Tiddly Winks—"Snap"—though we had animal names to say when we matched our cards—and I laughed myself sick and screamed, too, like murder every time I matched any badly. Leola and I almost came to blows. Then we played a game, the loser having to pay a forfeit by doing anything we named. So Herr Keller had to give us a skirt dance with a big checked apron on, and my plumed black hat! He is a good deal over six feet, and we simply howled, he was so ridiculous. Then Mlle. had to sing something. We had lots of fun—they just left and it must be nearly twelve o'clock.

Jan. 27

Madam Cranberry's birthday—lots of pretty flowers from friends. Grosse gave Fräulein something to drink—and after Fräulein had drunk all in her glass and had left—Grosse discovered she had given poor Fräulein pure cognac! I thought she acted queerly and looked rather rosy. The Parrot and her daughter came over this afternoon and was surprised they didn't make more "to do" about us not having been over to see them. ["The Parrot" and her daughter were probably neighbors, on whom Ima bestowed one of her whimsical nicknames.] This year the daughter played for us and played very well indeed, a Schumann Novelleten [Novelette]. Gerhard Goetze and a sister came over. Little Goetze is a cute funny little boy and I laughed heartily at him. We had birthday cake and goodies and then played games.

Jan. 28

Got to bed earlier—but lay awake almost all night—and today have been rather tired to do my work, but I practiced two hours and studied my German during the morning. This afternoon, I went to Pracht's for a shampoo. The three Thomases [probably neighbors] came tonight, Franz with the voice, August with the snaggle teeth, and Eduard with his little moustache. I meant to stay in my room and read a while and then go to beddie but came in nevertheless.

Jan. 29

In the morning, I wrote a letter to Xaver, telling him I couldn't take any more lessons! I hardly knew whether to do it or not, it has been worrying me for some time—I am not satisfied—and then one or two other reasons—quite good enough by themselves. Went out for a little walk later in the afternoon. Leola and Buddy went to see the "Magic Flute" and I stayed at home. Read a little and got sleepy by half past eight so went to bed—and when L & B returned at half past eleven, I felt like I'd had my night's rest.

Jan. 30

Had a letter from Brother telling me about an automobile accident he was in. The man next to him was instantly killed! I shudder to think of what chances we take with luck. Only the difference of being on a left seat instead of a right. Fräulein didn't come today. Went to the Kaufhaus des Westens and bought me a purple dress. Leola and I have decided to be more economical—cut out automobiles—I suppose that is the most extravagant thing we do.

Jan. 31

Today is Brother's birthday. Went to the Musik Handlung [music store] and bought a metronome. Dreadful weather—but Berlin always has ugly days—so few pretty bright days. Mr. Keller came tonight. We had egg-nog, as usual. Buddy and I played checkers, he beat me—Then Leola and I played and she beat me, too. Then Buddy and I had a very undignified encounter—pillow fight!—Am reading "Leopard Spots" by Thomas Dixon [followed by a drawing of something resembling a dandelion head].[29]

Buddy is an old dear, and makes life very interesting by telling me my faults—playing Truth. I try not to have my feelings hurt as I know it is all meant in good nature. Am very sorry to know, though, that my faults should give anybody so much pain or dismay and I shall endeavor to correct myself. I appreciate his interest. Yesterday, I told him I thought he'd been cross lately. He took it beautifully, but I'm afraid I hurt his feelings. He's really usually so sweet. I shouldn't have said anything. I wonder if I really did hurt his feelings? I'm awfully sorry if I did.

Feb. 1

Practiced on Becky [Bechstein piano] for the last time today.—They came and took her away this afternoon, and my poor little room looks so forlorn. Buddy and I have just finished playing some music together and Madam Cranberry is deaf and dumb, heart and soul on writing a story.—The Goetzes are nearly all of them sick with influenza.

Feb. 2

Breakfast at half past twelve. Mrs. Cranberry finished her story. I read some—the last part of "The Leopard's Spots." Studied German, but I don't think I'm doing very well in that.

Feb. 3

Fräulein couldn't come again. The mail man brought me from the Deutsche Vereinsbank in Munich forty-two marks, which they write me was due me on some American Express check they cashed for me last summer. As I had nothing to practice on, Mrs. C. and I went to town—first to exchange some opera tickets which were for a gala performance tonight—but owing to the assassination of the King of Portugal, the Royal Family will not attend. Next Monday, however, is another Gesellschaftsabend [a social or gala event]. Went to the Dresdner Bank and cashed $300.00 and proceeded to the Bristol for lunch. We certainly did enjoy, and felt absolutely sporty sitting up there so independently all alone. I invested in some stationery at a price I'm ashamed to name. The rest of the day was a blemish for me, spent it in running to piano houses hunting

for something fit to rent. Finally, went to Bechstein's and ordered a
new piano which is promised to arrive in the morning.

Tonight we have been telling our dreams of what we'd love to
have and do. May some of them come true. I dare not really think
of my future, heaven knows what luck it will hold—and I don't wish
to know. I rarely allow myself to think seriously of this—it doesn't
matter so much, anyhow.

Feb. 4

Becky the second arrived this morning, mighty good to see it sitting
in its little place in my room. We had had some fun over Buddy's
picture being found with its face turned to the wall. Each of us
swears he had nothing to do with it. Went to the dressmaker this
afternoon with my purple dress and had a hard time deciding how
to make it.

Went to Siegfried Wagner's concert with the Philharmonie.
The programme consisted of Richard Wagner's compositions and
the son's music of the same family as well in character. It is really
noble of Siegfried to compose after his father who has left such an
example.

Feb. 5

Have spent my day playing checkers with Mrs. C. and the Boy
[Buddy]. Was ignominiously defeated by both. But we've read
aloud too from Marie Corelli's "Free Opinions" and have started
her "Master Christian."[30] The latter is a story exceedingly well
written—so far—and has a most interesting theme.

Feb. 6

All got up late and Fräulein didn't come again. Practiced only a
little, Leola and I read a good part of the afternoon in "The Master
Christian." We went by for Helena Lewyn who has had tickets with
her for the Godowsky concert tonight. [Helena Lewyn was one of
many young music students in Berlin. She was a pupil of the noted
pianist and teacher Leopold Godowsky (1870–1938). She was from
Houston, where Ima may have known her.[31]]

As usual, the hall was crowded for him and a most enthusiastic

audience. He is a pianist after my own heart—I cannot think
of a thing which gives me a single unpleasant sensation, for as
unworthy as I am to do so, I dare to criticize anybody! Godowsky's
hands are very small indeed. But he plays Liszt as well as one with
regular Liszt hands, and such nuance and strength combined with
such daintiness and pianissimo. How anyone can say—as I've
heard people say—that he is merely a technical genius, I cannot
understand—for his insight into the music is to my mind most deep
and subtly so interpreted—

Herr Keller appeared this afternoon, took tea with us, was here
when we went to the concert, and was here when we returned.
Buddy and I have been spending the remainder of the evening
"fussing"—or something. At any rate, I've quite decided that
"familiarity breeds contempt." That I am full of faults I am not
unaware.—But I have never known anyone to take them and dissect
them so carefully for pastime. However, I'm also sure that he has
come to some conclusions which I feel aren't quite fair if he really
means everything he says seriously.

Feb. 7

Up late. Practiced a very little. Leola and I read a good part of the
afternoon. Gerhard Goetze came over and we all played ~~dominoes~~
checkers—at which I always lose. I cannot learn to play. Buddy and
I played a little music.

Feb. 8

Went to Arthur Schnabel's to see about taking lessons with him.
[Artur Schnabel was a Hungarian-born pianist and teacher, exactly
the same age as Ima Hogg.[32]] He was in Norway—but the maid
told me that he gave lessons for no less than two years. Have been
reading Imperial Germany by Sidney Whitman. Practiced a little.

Feb. 9

We are reading the New Testament now instead of "Imitation of
Christ." Mrs. Cranberry has been hard at her books all day—and
Buddy and I have been reading aloud to each other, most all
afternoon. First we read "The Beauties of Nature" by [Sir John]

Lubbock until I longed to be in some of the places I love in the country where I might enjoy some of the things I used to adore on the plantation. Sometimes I wish I had taken advantage more of the beautiful influences I had then when in West Columbia. I remember how I loved it all, too—but that it would never again be the same—!—. Grosse made us some egg-nog and then I read Buddy's story "The Lost Violin," a truly excellent piece of work. The plot is carried out well in the smallest detail and the English is carefully and well selected. It took me about two hours to finish the story and thinking it still early we had some music, Devil's Trill Sonata by Tartini, part of the violin concerto and Ballade Polonaise by Vieuxtemps.[33] Madam Cranberry during all this time had been absent and when she came in, we discovered it was after ten and we'd had no tea! Grosse was peacefully reposing on the couch all evening utterly unconscious of the passing time, too. I tied Buddy [in] a game of checkers, so memorable an event that I must put it down!

Feb. 10

Same kind of day as usually passed—only the weather was superb—a real rare thing in Berlin. We went to the opera Aida—The second Gesellschaftsabend again called off on account of death of some Duke. Destinn was Aida. Maclellan sang and we enjoyed the music.[34] The staging and costumes were magnificent.

Feb. 11

Woke up worn out after a perfect fully miserable night of frightful dreams, and the day, too, has been so dark and rainy that I've had a hard time doing anything. Had a note from Fräulein saying she'd been in the country visiting all this time that we've been wondering where she was. She will be here Thursday, though. Thank goodness. The music teacher, though, Schnabel comes to town tomorrow and I shall see if he won't take me. Buddy got a list from Halir and with the different objections we've heard to them—it has settled down to the two, Schnabel and Droucker, Sandra, the latter of whom I've never heard.[35] My paper came today—same monogram graphics which I ordered during a very extravagant moment, considering the price I paid for it—it is only fairly pretty—though I am real pleased

with the dainty lavender and the simple monogram. Gerhard
Goetze came over, stayed for tea, and was angrily sent for—these
German fathers are very stern and strict with their children.—He
has just returned and is this minute again sent for.

Feb. 12

Went to Schnabel again this morning but couldn't see him as he
had just returned from his tour and was resting in bed. Came home
upset and felt utterly hopeless. Finally decided to go to Dr. Martin
Krause and talk to him. [Martin Krause, a German pianist and
teacher who had studied under Franz Liszt, taught at the Stern
Conservatory in Berlin from 1896 to 1911.[36] He accepted Ima as a
private pupil.]

   He lives way out—had just moved there and had a hard time
locating him. But Buddy telephoned to his former place of living
for me—not without some hesitation—and demanded a kiss for
reward.—Well, Dr. Krause is a funny little man and I suppose I
might as well trust to luck and take my lessons from him. Augusta
Zuckermann, by the way, was playing something she composed at
his studio. I remember of hearing her play in New York long ago,
she was then a beautiful pianist.[37] Keller came and so did some of
the Goetzes. We all had a drawing. Keller drew Buddy and so did I.

Feb. 13

And Fräulein didn't come after all! The Sphinx [Leola] and I went
to a new Friseur [hairdresser] and were duly sorry—were simply
scalped. Then we went to the toy shop to buy something for the
little sick Ganz boy and bought pictures to color and the colored
pencils—came home and worked over them with all the earnestness
of a serious undertaking. Went to bed early and the Sphinx read to
me out of "The Master Christian."

Feb. 14

Back to Pracht's for a decent hair dressing. Went to Frederic
Lamond Chopin Abend [evening]—was not really worthwhile.
Grosse and Helena went instead of Buddy and Mrs. C. They went
to Carmen—with Strauss conducting, Destinn as "Carmen"—and

have just returned wild with enthusiasm—C. [Calvé] can't compare with D. [Destinn], etc.[38] Mrs. Grosse and I came in, we had no key to the front gate and I climbed the fence to ring the bell.—Today has been gorgeous—bright and cool. Some fine excitement we had late this afternoon—but mattered nothing.

Feb. 15

Went to Mr. Krause at half past four. I believe I am going to like him very much. I played a Chopin Nocturne for him—he was very nice about it. Gave me some suggestions about the playing of it— encouraged me a great deal by telling me at once that he saw I had unusual talent—and other things, too—though I don't care to start my lessons that way. Tonight the Sphinx and I almost finished the first volume of "The Master Christian" and then she told me in a very interesting way the story of "Vendetta" by Corelli.

Feb. 16

I spent the day playing checkers and reading. Finished first volume of "Master Christian." I simply don't know what I'm doing or thinking from playing checkers so much. I actually won two games from Leola and . . . another!!!!!

Feb. 17

The Fräulein didn't come, so I wrote her a letter suggesting that I would take no more lessons from her. Tonight we went to the Philharmonic Concert—Nikisch conducting—Gabrilowitsch the soloist.[39] He played a Rachmaninoff concerto for the piano—rather a thankless task, beautiful and yet with little interest as a concerto. In New York, I heard and admired Gabrilowitsch very much and am looking forward to hearing him in a recital here.—Grosse is sick with a bad cold. Madam and I have started on the second volume of "Master Christian."

Feb. 18

Got up late and had very little time to practice before lunch, and then had just time to take my soup before a mad dash for the American Consulate. Took an auto which fortunately appeared just

in time at the door as I went out and told the chauffeur I wanted to
get there before three—got there after—but was determined to sign
my papers there after having taken such ages to attend to it. Told the
droske man [droschke man, cab driver] to wait—wasn't gone very
long. Had to rewrite what Mr. T. had made out for me—only I did
have to change the date of my birth—which he had put years later![40]
Well, when I came out to find the auto—nowhere in sight. Couldn't
find him—and he hadn't been paid!! Got a car to the dressmaker's—
tried on my purple dress and then went over to Kaufhaus des
Westens for a little shopping—some of the Goetzes were over. Made
a handkerchief case for Leola.

Feb. 19

Spoke to Mademoiselle [Leola's French teacher] about asking a
friend of hers to come to me for a German lesson. Poor Fräulein
appeared this morning and has had a bad time with her eyes, lots of
good reasons for not coming to work, but suppose I might and will
take from somebody else.—The day is vile. Had my lesson with Prof.
Krause. Also paid him 80 marks for eight half hour lessons. But
today I had over an hour. Am going to start Bach. My little finger is
too stiff and my hand is not relaxed enough on my tone. He says I
must practice four hours every day—and it looks like he wants real
work. Took a car to Zoologischer Garten and then home again.—
    I feel like a dog—Buddy and I have barely spoken for several
days. I should be ashamed to take a child seriously, but I'm sure
I've allowed him to talk to me too much—and have treated him
altogether too familiarly—he has not understood—and I suppose
I've not been very nice either, still I cannot have my feelings hurt
by unkind things said—so I think nothing said is better. Still it is
hardly a good spirit to have in a home where one is the same as a
guest. I feel I really must be making things uncomfortable when
never in my life have I held such an attitude with people in their
own home. I am wicked—still—I do not think it is my place to say
anything. B. has said almost unpardonable things to me. I can not
think I deserve it all. Maybe I'll get good and make peace perhaps I
should. It's hard to be good—even if one knew how!

Feb. 20

My new German teacher came, and I am sorry to think what I've been missing all this time. She is fine. Practiced three hours, in fact, have been so busy the entire day that I am weary tonight. Leola and I have read all evening, too, in "The Master Christian." A glorious day.

Feb. 21

Another German lesson practiced again nearly three hours and then went to try on that tiresome dress. It was not right again so I left it to be changed. Mrs. Cranberry and I have read all evening.

Feb. 25

My lesson—Bach Prelude and Fugue, some Clementi, and a Chopin Nocturne. A letter came from Brother with sad news. Poor grandfather passed away some weeks ago, and Tom has been sent to Cuba![41] Such things it is but natural to grieve for, but being so far away makes the whole of life seem so dark. I should not write such things, still I'm sure it is a relief to express oneself rarely—and for that matter I could not half say in words the dreary things with which I am overcome. Only for the time, though, for I know Tom's removal is a means of advancement and that it is the first step to what seems a real separation—who knows how long before he'll be maybe in Japan and out of reach. It is hard to be brave—I'm afraid I'm not made of courage, however much I feel I have endured and with resignation. But these next few days—the last days of a month—of each day full of dear and painful remembrance—I can not altogether refuse to cherish the very things which hurt to remember. That I had known they were the last days.

Today, Brother's letter of the tenth came. Dear old bachelor—to his "Miss Ima" the sweetest of valentines came—"a wild violet, a fragrant jonquil, a plum blossom" all picked in the field on the plantation. This time two years ago I picked the last flowers there before saying farewell to the old place—and the old life—just before I went to Houston.

Fräulein came. I have practiced, but how well—?

"Two years ago" in the "last days" of February 1906 Ima Hogg had been with her father at Varner Plantation in West Columbia, Texas, the Hogg family's country home. On March 3, James Stephen Hogg died suddenly in Houston. His daughter still grieved.

Feb. 26

Leola and Buddy went to a Gesellschaftsabend. The entire Royal family were there—at the opera—all full dress. Mrs. C. gave a glowing description of the scene. Checkers and practice. Studied my German tonight. Bach is interesting but awfully ungrateful stuff to move on—that is—it takes longer to learn for me than anything—and I'm digging at it.

Feb. 27

German lesson and music, too. Krause says I have great talent for technic—a fact which is too comical for words and which I want to write so I can see it in black and white now and then when Bach seems a physical impossibility. He told me also today that three things were necessary in practicing—patience, the second patience, and the third likewise patience and that I had not one of the three. It's the truth. I am going to cut out fast playing, however, for one thing, and that will be a task which will certainly be a temptation resisted. Got a glimpse of Augusta Zuckermann in Krause's studio adjoining the music room. She had on a black Peter Thompson dress with a touch red and a red hat—she looked beautiful. I had not remembered her so.—

Met Mrs. C. at the Kaufhaus and we braved the terrors of a new dress apiece—the materials rather. Hers is tan pongee, and mine is a little deeper than turquoise blue. I hardly feel right in getting a color. I suppose I must some day, though.[42]

Feb. 27/8th

Practiced a new Fugue and Nocturne in D♭ major by Chopin. Went to Pracht's for a shampoo. Tonight we played cribbage. This morning, I told Leola all I thought about my conduct in connection with Buddy, about not speaking to him. She was lovely about it and seemed to understand. So I am relieved of her thinking that I am acting horridly in her home.

Feb. 28

German lesson—and practiced more than I have in a long time. Am getting crazy about Bach—and already I think I've gained by playing it. All of us played cribbage—and Grosse and I being partners—she is such a lucky one, we won.

Feb. 29

Lesson at half past twelve. Played the D♭ major Nocturne, Bach Prelude and Fugue in D major and Clementi Etude.[43] Took only two days to prepare these things in, I was not expecting to have a very good lesson, but I had practiced hard and did have a fair lesson. Mr. Krause, at any rate, was lovely to me and told me that he was "astonished at my talent"—I hesitate to write this, but I do like to remember it—and that isn't all he said, but quite enough.— Went with Helena Lewyn to a concert at Sing Akademie [a musical (originally choral) society].

Marie [space left blank] played Beethoven [blank] and Saint-Saëns [blank] concertos—a group of smaller pieces & for encore the Chopin Nocturne in D♭ major which I liked not at all. The first part she made quite broad and the last quite soft. The Saint-Saëns requires excellent technic—which she has and she played it with a dash and vim. Her principal good quality is powerful technic and lots of it. Helena told me tonight that Godowsky—her teacher—learned the Liszt E Concerto for a concert in Frankfurt—in <u>three days</u>!!!

Here, on the last day of February 1908 (February 29, a Leap Year), Ima Hogg's Berlin diary, which she began on January 1, ends, with no explanation. The little black *Tagebuch* with its brass lock has many unused pages. Why did Ima suddenly stop keeping a diary? She lived at Mommsenstrasse 22 (except for part of the summer) until October 1908, when she sailed for home. What did she do from March to October? Surviving documents are few.

On March 9 and 13 she went to concerts: "Mozart Saal," March 9; "Philharmonie," March 13. There are programs with these dates in her scrapbook, but she did not say who, if anyone, accompanied her.

On April 13 Ima's brother Tom wrote to her at the Mommsenstrasse 22 address: "So you have a secret to tell me one of these days, well look here little sis, don't you know, I won't stand for your having secrets and not telling your buddy Thomas of them, for it looks kind of suspicious, Sabe? So you had better tell me, poco tempi, sabe?"[44] Tom could be very persuasive. Ima's reply, like most of her letters, has not survived. Neither has her "secret."

There is no record of concertgoing, music lessons, or any other activities for Ima Hogg from mid-March until late May. On May 17 Leola's mother arrived in Berlin to join Leola, Henry, Selma White (their grandmother), and Ima at Mommsenstrasse 22. They planned a summer in Germany's Harz Mountains, a famous resort area, and asked Ima to join them. Meanwhile, Ima had at least one more music lesson.

On May 29 Martin Krause sent her a postcard:

> Dear Miss Hogg!
>
> I hope you know, I expect you today at half past five.
> Best wishes
>
> M. Krause[45]

Did Ima appear for this lesson? On June 14, 1908, Ima's friend John E. Green Jr., age twenty-seven, a bachelor attorney in Houston, wrote to her at the Charlottenburg address.[46] Sometime in late June or early July, Ima and the Fisher family left Berlin for the Harz Mountains. In the Ima Hogg Papers in Austin, there is a photograph of Ima and a young man. On the back of the photo, in Ima's handwriting, is "Harz Mts." The young man's identity is unknown.

On July 12 the *Houston Post* reported receiving letters from Ima Hogg and Leola Fisher, who were vacationing in Germany. Ima planned "to come home in October." They evidently stayed in the Harz Mountains through most of August. On August 19 a Houstonian, Ben Weems Jr., wrote to the Decatur, Texas, *Wise County Messenger* that he had joined Ima Hogg and the "H. F. Fisher family" in the Harz Mountains.

By September Ima was again in Berlin and attending concerts on September 12 and 17. She was planning a return to Houston. The Fishers remained in Germany. On October 6 Ima sailed from Bremen on the *Kaiser Wilhelm der Grosse*, arriving in New York on October 13.[47]

Figure 8. Ima Hogg and unknown young man, Harz Mountains, 1908

Home in Houston at last, after an absence of sixteen months, Ima soon resumed her busy social schedule. On October 29, 1908, the *Houston Post* reported that Ima Hogg was attending the Dallas Fair. She spent much of November visiting friends and attending parties in Austin, and in December she was the house guest of Helen (Mrs. Lewis) Thompson, her 1907 travel companion, in Houston. According to the *Houston Post*, Ima planned to spend Christmas with her brother Will at Varner Plantation. Early in January 1909 Ima was back in Houston, staying at the home of Mrs. H. F. Fisher—Leola's mother. Leola and Henry and their grandmother were still in Berlin. Ima was evidently not yet settled into a residence in Houston but staying with various friends. In May the *Houston Post* reported that Ima was "now with Mr. & Mrs. Snyder Carlton, 1617 McGowen." Snyder Carlton was a business partner of Will Hogg's, and the Carltons were longtime family friends. By October 1909 Ima and Will were in "apartments for the winter in the Warrington" at 1502 Fannin.[48] Mike Hogg was finishing his law degree at the University of Texas, and Tom was still in the Marines. Ima and Will later moved to another apartment in the Oxford at 1402 Fannin, where they would live for the next few years.

After her travels and study abroad, Ima immersed herself in social and cultural activities in Houston. She began giving piano lessons to a select handful of students.[49] Regretfully, she gave up her dream of becoming a concert pianist. She once told a close friend that the great sorrow of her life was that she "was never a concert pianist." Because her hands were small, she knew she lacked the wide keyboard reach that a first-rank artist should have. She did have, as her friend Nettie Jones recalled, "a bone-crushing grip." But Ima Hogg did not give up her attachment (whatever it was) to Germany. Some years after Ima Hogg's death, Mary Fuller, a friend of Ima's since the early 1900s, said that after Ima returned from her year abroad, she "was not interested in men." Was that because she had a secret romance in Germany? Fuller also said that Ima never went to Europe without visiting Germany.[50] Ima Hogg would visit there periodically for the rest of her life.

3

Travels with Mike

1910

In the summer of 1910 Ima sailed again for Europe, this time with her brother Mike. She was twenty-eight; Mike, twenty-five. This item appeared in the *Galveston Daily News*, July 1, 1910:

> Friends of Miss Ima Hogg of Houston, who gathered at the North German Lloyd pier Thursday to bid Miss Hogg and her brother, Mr. Mike Hogg, bon voyage on their departure for Europe, noted with pleasure the pretty courtesy paid by the tug *Ima Hogg*. When the ocean liner was leaving the pier the tug named for this daughter of the late Governor Hogg drew alongside the *Hanover* and gave a salute of three whistles while passing around the vessel upon the deck of which stood the fair lady whose namesake the tug is. Miss Hogg was pleased with the pretty compliment, and smilingly waved a good-by to those whose thought prompted the salute.

Ima Hogg would never escape her name. But she was sailing to Germany, where "Ima Hogg" was pronounced "ee-ma hock," and even if the English pronunciation, "eye-ma hog," were known, nobody would think of it as "I'm a" (in German "ich bin ein"). And nobody would associate "Hogg" with a "Schwein." No wonder she liked to be among Germans. In the slender black notebook she had used for her 1907 travels (Why

did she not use the nearly-empty 1908 diary?) Ima recorded her travels
with her brother Mike.

> *From Galveston to Bremen via "Hanover" N.G.L.*
> *Sailed June 30 arrived July 18, 1910*
> A most pleasant voyage with a very jolly and interesting number of
> passengers.

Also sailing aboard the *Hanover* were Laura Franklin, two years older
than Ima, a Houston friend since the early 1900s, and Laura's widowed
mother.[1] Ima makes no mention of these two in her diary.

> This time I am attempting to "conduct" a party—of two—Mike and
> myself. So far we have not gotten on the wrong train, our tickets have
> been good, and nothing outside the experiences Mike and I create
> for ourselves has occurred. Our tickets, second class, from Berlin to
> London were $18.00 apiece
>   A short account of our trip would be as follows.

This account is even shorter because it omits the first twelve days of
the trip: the days Ima and Mike spent in Berlin. Their ship docked at
Bremen on July 18. Then they traveled to Berlin, where they remained
until July 31. Where they stayed, what they did there, and whom they
saw there are not recorded. Ima had not been in Berlin since October
1908. One imagines that she would want Mike to see Mommsenstrasse
22, where she had lived for nearly a year. One imagines that she would
want to see Leola Fisher, who had married Siegfried Goetze just a few
months earlier, on March 10, 1910. Surely Ima and Mike visited the
newlyweds. Leola's grandmother, Selma White ("Grosse" in Ima's 1908
diary), was still in Berlin, although quite ill. She died on July 23, while
Ima and Mike were presumably still there. Did Ima visit her, perhaps
attend her funeral?

What was so private, so secret, about Ima's time in Berlin in 1908 that
she did not record anything of her return visit in 1910? That visit merited
only a single, terse line in her diary: "Left Berlin Sunday [July 31] 10:55
A.M." The rest of this diary is a routine travel journal. Departing Berlin,
Ima and Mike went that same day to Cologne.

Arrived Cöln [Köln] 9:00 P.M.

Hotel here 4 M. [German Marks] bed and breakfast each—very good. After seeing the Cathedral went to the Church of St. Ursula with the bones of the 10,000 virgins used to decorate the walls. Took a drive through the city and along the Rhine. Raining. Lost umbrella. Bought another.

Left Cöln [Köln] Monday [August 1] 2:30 P.M.
Arrived Brussels 9:30 P.M.

Fair was going on. And here we had the most terrible experience.— We could find no place to stay. All the good—and then indifferent hotels were "full up."[2] Finally, as a final resort we went to the Metropole here—we thought it would be impossible to get anything—and we found a place for 12 F. [Belgian francs] apiece. The next morning we had a glimpse of the gallery, a beautiful drive through the Exhibition grounds, a walk through indifferently interesting exhibits, then lunch. Mike was disgusted with the city and so was I. We had a pleasant walk through the "old place"— where are the buildings—Hotel de Ville etc.

The second umbrella was left on the train, and as it was raining, bought <u>No 3</u>.

Left Brussels Tuesday [August 2] 4:15 P.M.
Arrived Bruges 6:25 P.M.

Hotel du Londres 3.50 Fr. a bed, table d'hôte meals, excellent and moderate prices. We had a little walk after dinner.

The next morning [Wednesday August 3] we continued our walk through the old streets, and over the canals, enjoying the same quaint Gothic houses, the picturesque views at every crooked turn. The Belfry, the many churches and cathedrals give a beautiful outline to the roofs of the little town. We went to the Hospital St. John where I again marveled at the exquisite workmanship and the beauty of Memling's pictures: The Legend of St. Ursula, Adoration of the Magi, and the Marriage of St. Catherine, etc. Mike, too, enjoyed these pictures as no others he has seen I think, with perhaps the exception of some in the Tate Gallery in London. <u>Umbrella No. 4.</u>

Left Bruges 2:10 for Ostend
Sailed for Dover 3:30 arrived 6 P.M.
Arrived Canterbury Wednesday 9:30 P.M.

Hotel Statler's Temperance 6 shil[lings] pension, a very good, unpretentious place. The Cathedral, the close, and the ruins behind the cathedral make a very impressive whole. This cathedral is a transition example of perpendicular Gothic and with the Norman influence. The raised choir is exceptional and very lovely. I shall never forget the view from Mercery Lane, from the corner where it is said the Inn stood at which the Canterbury Pilgrims halted—(Chaucer). I found Canterbury well worth a long stay. We had here an interesting walk along High Street.

Soldiers—fine specimens—passed in long procession on bicycle—and fresh wholesome boys in characteristic school costume filled the street as it was commencement day at the fine preparatory school here.

Left Canterbury Thursday [August 4] 2:20
Arrived London 5:20 P.M.

Drove (2/6) to Torrington Sq. where we found board (6/6) no lunch—clean rooms, nice people, poor food. In London we did the usual things. This time I enjoyed Temple Courts (Middle Temple), Wallace Collection, Kensington Museum, Cheshire Cheese Inn, walk through Fleet Street, Hampton Court boat at 4:30 to Richmond—walk up to the hill—gorgeous never to be forgotten view with sunset, and a fine dinner. Home by train and subway. At the Japanese-British Exhibit we saw the Japanese wrestlers, a great novelty and a strange thing, too.

Heard Tetrazzini at Opera in Barber of Seville. Saw "Priscilla Runs Away." Wilson-Terry (charming)—"The Whip"—thrilling melodrama, but good. Am sorry I didn't start this sooner for now I am trying to catch up and can not feel like taking time to tell the things which I have felt most important. Here's one thing, we are seeing the life of the people—as upon the Thames, where were the house-boats, etc. as I did not before. The week of Cricket at Canterbury—National Festival—We went down Thursday. A

wonderful sight and experience it was; throngs of enthusiasts
who were self contained—, a brilliant sight on the velvety big area
of green. A most scientific game is cricket but a very unexciting
performance, I think.

Left London Aug. 8 Monday, 2:30. Arrived Windsor by train
(Paddington) 3:20 P.M. White Hart rooms 5/6—meals most
expensive and an air of graft which irritated me.—Viewed the castle
and very imposing grounds.

Left Tuesday at 2:30 P.M. for steam boat trip on the Thames—to
Henley—arrived 7:15 P.M.

This trip is decidedly not to be missed—

The beautiful homes and the estate of Astor—Cliveden—are
a sight perhaps nowhere else to be seen in just in such a state of
symmetrical beauty. The flowers particularly were so profuse and
gay in color on the perfect lawns.

Arrived in Oxford 9:45 P.M.

Mike and I both cold and head-aching. And here was the evil-
charm, the land which I shall not mention, as I hope to forget such
a place exists. No—I do not for it was an <u>event</u> I shall likely never
see in such another similar sphere. We did not stay long on that
account. But we drank in the dear old town, apart in its beauty. The
day was superb—sunny, and mild.

[written in the margin of this page:]

"The Light of the World" W. H. [William Holman] Hunt
Keble College Glorious masterpiece

What "evil charm," what "event" did Ima mean? Once again, Ima Hogg
was good at keeping some things to herself. She had not been to Oxford
since 1907, when she had described its colleges and environs in glowing
terms: "How I long to get back to Oxford, once again.—<u>Diary</u>, July 11,
1907."

In August 1910 she remembered something unpleasant at Oxford that
disturbed her. She did not record the name of the hotel where she and
Mike stayed or any details of their visit. They spent one night.

Left Oxford Wednesday 2:15 P.M.
Arrived Warwick 3:30

Dale's Temperance Hotel (Excellent Rooms 2/3—Meals delicious
& moderate) (Could take train) Cab 1/6. I had a room here, in the
Annex—a quaint, old house. The bed and the other furniture were
of magnificent solid mahogany, of that clear light colored wood so
rare in our country. We went through the castle grounds and the
castle. The guide told us that the Earl and Countess would return
the next day with an immense party (100 he said) so the castle
would be closed to visitors.[3] I later learned that these two live very
extravagantly and are not rich, either. I suppose five shillings which
comes with every visitor helps a little!

Thursday morning 10:20 Stratford

It was warm and the town has not grown in my favor since 1907.
We visited Shakespeare's birthplace and then his burial in the
church. At the Golden Lion (starred in 1906 Baedeker) we had an
insufficient and poor lunch @ 2/6 and in disgust with everything
returned to Warwick on the 2:08 train. That afternoon we read
and wrote. I reviewed "Kenilworth." After our delicious dinner,
we walked out to the bridge near the castle. It was some sort of a
holiday—a brass band was playing discords, and a happy, well-
behaved crowd were running and pushing the poor performers
along.

Off Friday morning 10:08
Went by trolley then to Milverton[4]
Arrived in Kenilworth 10:40

Drove a mile and a half to the castle 6 d. [sixpence] These romantic
and very beautiful ruins we saw to the best advantage, for after a
walk about them, we drove on the way to the station, with the tilting
ground, had a fine view of the whole castle, where the lake used to
be. Merwyn Tower was the scene of Amy's life in the castle.

Amy Robsart, wife of Robert Dudley, Earl of Leicester, is the heroine of
Walter Scott's novel *Kenilworth*, which Ima had just "reviewed" the day
before. "In Warwick, by the way, he & the Earl of Leicester are buried."

Left Kenilworth 12:25 noon

After innumerable changes arrived in Ambergate at 4:30 P.M. to find that we should have to go farther in order to coach to Haddon Hall, & Chatsworth. We spent the time there until 6:18 P.M.— walked, drank tea and admired this promising beginning of the Peak—Bought tickets to Rowsley, but decided to get off in Matlock, 6:40 P.M. A mountainous and beautiful place—and a nice hotel— "New Bath"—with a pleasant garden.—So many of the lower classes seem to be traveling hereabouts—just tiny little journeys. There is a grand piano here in Matlock.—I am aching to <u>touch it</u>!

This was Friday, August 12, 1910. Here the diary ends. The little notebook has more blank pages, but Ima did not use them. What did she and Mike do on the rest of their journey? On September 4, 1910, the *Houston Post* received a letter from Ima in Scotland, saying that "she is coming home in October." On October 10, 1910, the *Galveston Daily News* reported that "Miss Ima Hogg is home after a delightful summer abroad."

Ima came home to a busy social life in Houston. She kept up her musical interests, joining the Women's Choral Club, helping found the Girls' Musical Club in 1911, and continuing to teach and mentor a few piano pupils. She moved into her own apartment in the Beaconsfield at 1700 Main Street, an eight-story building that opened in 1911 as Houston's first high-rise apartment building.[5] In early 1912 Ima Hogg was initiated into the Austin chapter of Pi Beta Phi, an international women's fraternity, and in April 1912 she joined the Episcopal Church as a member of Houston's Christ Church Cathedral community.[6]

In the summer of 1912 Ima went abroad again: She spent three months traveling in Europe from July to September. If she kept a diary this time, it has not been located. She sailed from Galveston on the *Hanover* on June 30 with two friends, Laura Franklin and Mary Elizabeth Rouse. The *Houston Post* reported that they "planned to spend about two months in Munich in musical study" and then visit Paris. Both young women were Ima's age and, like her, unmarried. Laura Franklin was the youngest of six children. Her Irish father had owned a "dry goods" store in Houston. Laura was a Houston socialite and, like Ima, a friend of Alice MacFarland. In 1910 Laura and her widowed mother had sailed to Germany on the *Hanover* with Ima and Mike Hogg. Mary Elizabeth Rouse was a young music teacher with her own studio at 2717 Main Street in Houston.[7] She would be a valuable asset to Ima in 1913 when Ima worked to found the Houston Symphony Orchestra and would travel with her to Germany in 1914. Where this trio went, and what they did, for three months in Europe can be partially gleaned from Ima's indefatigable program notes: In Germany, at Bayreuth, *Der Ring des Nibelungen,* and in Munich, more Wagner operas.

Ima and Laura Franklin sailed home at the end of September, arriving in New York on the *Victoria Louise* on October 5, 1912.[8] Mary Elizabeth Rouse is not on that passenger list, and her travel schedule is not known. She was back in Houston in plenty of time to help Ima put together a symphony orchestra. Ima Hogg's lifelong passion was music, and one of her proudest achievements was the Houston Symphony, which played its first concert on June 21, 1913.[9]

4

The Great War Begins

1914

In the summer of 1914, Ima Hogg, who had lived in Germany in 1907–8 and had traveled to Europe in 1910, 1911, and 1912, suddenly decided to go abroad again. In Houston on July 10, 1914, Ima's eldest brother, Will, wrote in his diary: "Miss I proposes to go to Europe." The very next day he wrote, "Miss I and I take Interurban [the train from Houston to Galveston] at 1 pm for her to take 'Chemnitz' . . . for Bremen."[1] Will's diary does not comment further. His sister, attractive but still unmarried at age thirty-two, was active in Houston's social life, a founder of the Houston Symphony, and a teacher of piano to a select group of pupils. To this day, the reason for her impulsive journey remains unclear. She sailed from Galveston on a German ship of the North German Lloyd line, the *Chemnitz*, on July 11, bound for the port of Bremerhaven.

On June 28, Archduke Franz Ferdinand, heir to the Austro-Hungarian throne, and his wife, Duchess Sophie, had been assassinated by a Serbian dissident in Sarajevo. While the *Chemnitz* was still at sea, diplomatic dominoes across Europe were tumbling down. Apprehensive passengers aboard the *Chemnitz* stayed informed of the news by cable. On July 28, Austria declared war on Serbia, and Russia began to prepare for war against Austria. On July 31, Germany sent a stern warning to Russia. On August 1, the day that the *Chemnitz* arrived in Bremerhaven, Germany

Figure 9. 1914 diary

declared war on Russia. World War I was about to begin.[2] Two days later, Ima Hogg began this diary in a "dear little book" she bought in Bremerhaven.

Aug. 3 1914, Hook of Holland[3]

Guarded by Holland Men of War. We are on the St. Petersburg at anchor ready to cross of [to] England[4]—quiet and some sense of security seem within short reach. August the first we arrived at Bremerhaven on the good ship Chemnitz from Galveston[5]—a voyage of twenty-one days. We were in a measure prepared for the terrible news which greeted us that Germany and Russia were mobilizing. Our ship four or five days ahead had kept us informed in a measure of the conditions ensuing from the Austro-Servian [sic] war news. At present I am really too fatigued and distressed to be writing. However, the atmosphere is such that one does not feel like quietly turning in for much needed rest. From the moment we arose Saturday morning at five, on the Chemnitz until the present moment, has been one succession of shocks and strain. We were until half past nine being allowed to get off the ship. We were astonished to see German guards up and down the wharfs, to prevent Russians from landing.

Chemnitz passengers were quickly escorted aboard a train for the city of Bremen, thirty-five miles to the south. En route, Ima looked out the train's windows and comforted herself by admiring the scenery.

My eyes were rejoiced all the way from Bremerhaven to Bremen by the beautiful fields and the rosy faced toilers which I have long ago learned to love. Germany has never looked lovelier to my eyes or the Germans sturdier and finer. What a superb land and people! On getting to Bremen I made as fast as I could to Hotel Central for rooms for Miss Rouse, Ruth Curtis and myself.[6] I was surprised to get rooms and that the prices were not raised in view of the great rush there from all points. But the real rush began right after we had secured our rooms. The German Kaiser had made an ultimatum to Russia that if she did not cease her mobilization she [Germany] would by night declare a formal mobilization. By

three o'clock I think it was that we got news that Russia would not
accede to Germany's demands. I have since read the telegrams
of the Kaiser and the Czar in which they share marked anxiety
to prevent a clash. The Czar, though, said that the feeling was so
bitter and great in his country that he did not see how he could go
against popular will. Our hotel was directly across from the Haupt
Bahnhof [Hauptbahnhof, main railway station], so we could see the
companies starting off in their fine trim and the beautiful officers.
The big square in front of the station was crowded with spectators
and members of families of the off-going soldiers. There were few
cheers during the day, though at night we heard national songs and
some show of life. The current of excitement was so restrained—and
yet evident, that all foreigners made plans to leave immediately.
The train left at four for London and I was for going with many
others—not that I was the least fearful, only I felt the trains would
probably be cut off for outside travel and we would be caught in
a country which began to look rather helpless to me. Ruth and I
walked in the afternoon to the Rath Haus [town hall] district. I was
afterwards glad we decided to remain over, though now the memory
makes my heart very heavy. Everything seemed suspended. The
streets were crowded with Germans walking about in a dazed way
with such serious, anxious faces and gathered in the public squares
by the Rath Haus tensely discussing the situation. Official bulletins
were plastered on corners for them to read and all orders for
mobilization on red papers. Already the panic for food was abroad.
In some shops they told me everyone had been laying in a supply
for food—no potatoes to be had even then—and small change was
not to be had. The organization—the control of telegraph cables,
the press, every wheel in the machinery of this military government
was at once set into motion. It was not long before proclamations
put a limit on the price of food stuffs. I went to send a cable—no
codes—and I had to send my message in German. I don't think it
ever got off either.

I bought several little things while in Bremen, this book [a
small cloth-covered journal], some pretty blotters, two rubber
balls for my two little god-sons. Nobody would take large money.
The banks were closed and we were quite tight for money. I was

desirous of buying a trunk. My old one was broken to pieces, so
I found a nice place where they took American Express checks. I
got a big German "hand-trunk" and lucky I did for it is now all I
have with me. In all the shops I talked with the people. They were
very unwilling to have war and if I am any judge of faces the whole
population looked unwilling. They are patriotic, these Germans,
but they love their families and their beautiful land more than
they do their government. I never met a German <u>in</u> Germany who
would express dissatisfaction. Outside they weren't as loyal. They
say in Berlin the anti-war demonstrations were very exciting,
however. When I lived in Berlin the Socialist-democrats were always
assembling on Sundays before the Kaiser's palace. Well, when
Sunday morning [August 2] came the porter at our hotel strongly
advised our leaving. Many of the men in the restaurant had already
gone to join the army. Ruth and I went to the American consul for
a passport. Of course all Americans were crowding in there. John
Lee, the consul, had been steadily issuing certificates for days and
among the excited countrymen and the names he had to give, he
was calmness itself, and courteous as in a drawing room. It took a
long time to get our turn and with the certificates we got advice to
get out to London at once. It was then late, so we went to the hotel
and told Miss Rouse, and at last made her feel the necessity for
immediate action. The McClendons happened along just in time,[7]
so at four o'clock a big crowd of the <u>Chemnitz</u> passengers started
for London. I crammed a large part of my things into my big bag—
not enough, as I now realize, for there was neither time nor space
for our trunks, so I had to leave two at the hotel with a great deal
which was valuable. All of us seemed rattled, and I think none of us
realized the true situation. The wagons were packed with English,
Dutch, Americans, Germans, Armenians, and even Russians, many
without passports. It was like a common family, each one helping
the other. All had varying experiences to relate, and we were not
long in deciding we were going in the right direction. Four hours we
traveled without stopping—through villages where at each station
great anxious strained faces were huddled together. Then we began
making stops and we began to fear we'd be turned out for soldiers.
But by night, rather late, too, we got to Osnabrück near the border.

The Englishmen were terribly worried. But for some inexplicable reason the officers troubled themselves very little about those in our train. In our wagon they merely looked in at us several times. In Holland they put us like cattle into any kind of trains. A third class <u>wagun</u> [wagon, train car] fell to our lot, and through the night we sat on the hard benches. Some English people, Mr. & Mrs. Elder, who had been with us off and on, kept us wide awake. Mr. Elder was wonderfully good. The small attentions during this long anxious journey I shall never forget. Men I never saw but for a moment took my bag down or would carry it, or would give their seat to one of us, or get us food. We reached Rotterdam at 5:30 A.M. Monday [August 3]. Our train had changed its route from time to time and we had gotten in and out of trains until we never knew where we were going. Our hardships were nothing to compare to those of others who went later or before. I suppose Sunday being so difficult to get money for tickets had kept us from being so jammed. They say [in] the trains from Berlin people crushed each other if one moved, and the officials were very rude and strict. The further we got from Germany the worse tales we heard! At every point we were told we could go no further, and that the boats would not sail from Hook of Holland. Food was almost impossible to buy. The little Dutch soldiers were mobilizing—such babies. And I think they were much more rattled than the Germans. Such rumors as were given us! The French were burning Paris—a Revolution was taking place—the Kron Prinz [Crown Prince] was killed—the Germans would capture our vessel if we attempted to cross the Channel. Of course we did not believe these things, but the doubt which balked every step was very wearing. We stayed in the station at Rotterdam never knowing when we could leave. [We] left at 11:30 A.M. They got us into a train for the Hook. The boat left at midnight packed and jammed. We got berths luckily, and I fell into bed about 6:30 [A.M.], not before having some hot soup and a little food.

Ima and many others were at last safely aboard the *St. Petersburg*, bound for Harwich, England.

[Aug. 4,] London

Tuesday morning about ten-forty we got to Liverpool street station. Wild crowds clambered into the wagons at Harwich. There really weren't enough carriages in the long train to accommodate all who had fled on the boat across from Holland. Relieved minds, though, to be once more on English-speaking soil. We hoped to know some of the real situation. The notices were posted all over Rotterdam proclaiming absurd and impossible things. I wonder if the French air ships did drop bombs over Nuremberg?[8] At the station in Rotterdam flocks of Germans came in on trains going back at the call of their country. Most of them were speaking good English and looked to be of very good class. In our carriage was Kitty Cheatham, the singer.[9] She was very friendly, and at once entered into conversation with those in the compartment. She had come from Weimar; she had been advised to leave within two hours, and had packed her music and a part of her things in various parcels, and had caught the train and traveled also since Saturday without laying her head on a pillow. [She] had not been undressed since then. She reminded us that Fritz Kreisler was an officer in the Austrian army. How many there are of those great ones who have no business fighting![10]

At the station here Mr. Elder once more turned guardian angel, phoned to the Hotel Imperial, Russell Square, and got accommodations for the McClendons and us. The hotel is immense. A panicky crowd greeted us in the lobby. I think we got about all [the rooms] they had left. I don't know what the papers had been printing here but they are as enterprising in springing surprises on the gullible public as our American "journals." Lord Grey had just made his speech and Great Britain had received its ultimatum also from Germany.[11] Midnight the answer was given that Great Britain would not remain neutral. Germany was on Belgian soil.

On Tuesday, August 4, England declared war on Germany. Ima and her companions attended an antiwar meeting in London that very night.

The women were having a speaking in Kingsway Hall against war that night, and we went. Most thrilling was the meeting. Women from Germany, Austria, Russia and the unions of England spoke. All spoke from their hearts, and denounced the diplomacy of nations claiming the degree of civilization Europe does. [They] said it was a war imposed by a few men upon peace loving nations. Olive Schreiner sat next [to] the Chairman and many names I heard there were well known.[12]

While we were listening to cries for peace down around Whitehall and Buckingham, London was awaiting its sentence. Great demonstrations of enthusiasm were accorded those who were to involve this country. As for me, I was stunned. We went to the American Express for some money. Here also the banks were closed: continuation of Aug. 1st Bank Holiday. The American Express was doing all it could for its patrons—forty dollars was the limit to each person. Of course the line was a continuous performance. They limited the hours. Those first two days were spent as in a dream. The foreigners here were many of them in need because as far as I could learn the American Ex. was the only exchange to be had. At once the influential Americans and the rich took steps to relieve their countrymen. The Savoy was headquarters for information, help of all kinds. Everybody registered. I don't know what good will come of it. As yet most of us have no prospects of getting home. All lines have stopped—for purposes of war. All German and English ships are in service. Now we recall that the <u>Chemnitz</u>, two days before landing was being painted dark gray, and that in Baltimore whereas we were to have spent only a few hours there we spent the day and night in coaling. Evidently this thing was being prepared for if not altogether expected, which reminds me of the frowning expression of the English Channel as we passed through to Germany [en route to Bremerhaven on the Chemnitz]. Seventeen men of war were lined up as we went by. The sun those two last evenings I shall never forget. With the news of probable war on our minds, the sunset was more impressive. It looked like a half eclipse, blood-red, sinking behind a long stretch of thick black cloud. All the rest of the sky was clear and the water was smooth enough to reflect a long streak of blood-red. I've looked for the sunset all my life, but a stranger more ominous sight I've never beheld. In the North Sea torpedo-boats and men of war gave the sun the same setting and it sank red and in half behind the same line of black cloud as in the Channel. Sometimes, I am optimistic about the outcome enough to think it cannot go on. At other times when I allow my feelings to get the better of my reason, I shiver. I suppose that is because I went through a period of nerve-wracking doubt before I left home. The night before I left home I suffered unreasoning fear of a kind I never knew possible. I had wanted to come to Europe this summer but could never make myself plan for it. It was only the Friday before the sailing that I tried to make myself—I wanted to come—and something in me feared and cried out against it. Surely, nothing has happened to justify a feeling of superstition. So far I wouldn't exchange anything for this experience. I have seen the hearts of people of two nations, and of crowds such as I never dreamed they had, and I have seen great nobility through it all. The world is better and finer than I dreamed.

As the days passed, Ima and her companions settled into life in London, where they would spend the next six weeks.

The tension here seems to be relieved. For days the great streams of people were full of war news and bewilderment. The government here as in Germany is to be congratulated on one thing: its mastery of organization. Here confidence is restored. People eat again without fear and the faces are reflecting a satisfaction and certainty of the future. I for one can at least think and look for something occasionally outside of the "latest." The first two days [Tuesday and Wednesday, August 4 and 5] we [illegible] between the American Committee at the Savoy and American Express. The rich Americans lost no time in trying to relieve their fellow countrymen. Some rushed home steerage. There is no rushing now. There seems to be no way to rush out anywhere.

All of us went to the Coliseum one night for vaudeville. Intermission was prolonged into a half hour of demonstration to cheer pictures of the King, Balfour, Grey, and Kitchener.[13] The Czar of Russia was hissed by a few—we being among the "few." Then everybody sang "God Save the King," and we, "My Country 'Tis of Thee."

Thursday, [August 6] we went to Westminster—Mrs. McClendon, Ruth and myself, and then to the Army and Navy stores where we had a nice lunch. Afterwards we walked through Haymarket and Regent. The shops looked very inviting. We bought some gloves at Peter Robinson's. There are two. The one on Regent is dearer, as we found out. When we got back to the hotel, I ran into Miss Mary Hubbard Smith.[14] Ten years dropped from my shoulders! The last time we saw her she had boarded the train for Cöln [sic; Cologne] instead of Amsterdam, in Bremen. All the time she had been enjoying herself in Amsterdam—got there somehow. We had been so worried about her. That night she and Mary E. Rouse and I went to "Monna Vanna" with Constance Collier.[15] For 2/6 [two shillings, sixpence] we got seats in the pit—a comfortable and inexpensive way in London of seeing good plays. Maeterlinck ever exquisite and lofty, is at his best in this play, and the acting, combined with wonderful subtle color effects was entrancing. The whole atmosphere made one feel the exaltation of some inspired orchestra music. Constance Collier was particularly fine. Saturday night we saw "Kismet," very good, more pleasing, for this one part of the beggar Hadge (?) [Haji]—such scenic effects. Sunday [August 9] Miss Smith and I attended part of the service at St. Paul's in jams of people. We got tired and left, getting our places on top of the hospitable bus.

We went by Westminster and were just in time to see a large company of soldiers march with wagons and provisions, I'm sure to some point of mobilization. We went back to Charing Cross and at Morley's had a refreshing luncheon (2/6). Once again we got on "top a bus" and went into Hyde Park walking around where the band was playing and then over to Buckingham Palace. The crowds had been around all day shouting for the King. We waited a long time and finally a modest little brown carriage drawn by two horses brought out the queen. No one cheered her. By this time it was late enough for tea so we had wonderful tea and refreshment at Ritz's (2/6). Mr. E. S. Thorpe, a Texas Englishman, was staying in our hotel. We happened upon each other at the door. He wanted to go out somewhere, so on top a bus we got! He says I have "busitis." All London was out. Every street had streams of people.

At Westminster we got down and joined the crowd going toward Buckingham again. Here they were thick as possible. We stood in the shouting masses—for an hour and a half hoping with them that the royal family would appear. Popular songs, patriotic songs, jests—such a carnival spirit was abroad! We got tired and started to wend our way out. Acres and acres, we wedged through, and then as far as eyes could reach they were massed. Turning home as far as Russell Square it was the same way. London on Sunday has always seemed to me like the dead. Little boys were marching in groups, mock soldiers beating tin cans, carrying "The flag." In every direction one met soldiers and the fine looking Scotch kilties.

Monday morning [August 10] Miss Smith, Mrs. Greg Leavell and I ventured into Rag Market over near Aldgate.[16] It is a filthy district and we found the market not worth while for week days. I lunched at Selfridge's, very nice things to eat. Mr. Thorpe and I tried to get into the gallery of Parliament but the plans didn't pan out and we made up our minds to go if possible when the session starts in the last of the month.

On August 11 Ima, Mary Elizabeth Rouse, and Ruth Curtis took a side trip to Cambridge, where they explored the university and the town for three days.

Aug. 13, Cambridge

The view before me is like nothing else I've known. The River Cam at my feet, the ages-old trees, the venerable, beautiful college buildings, and the young students enjoying the boating. Many are reading, or I presume studying, as they idle along in the canoes, a pipe hanging in one side of the mouth. Trinity is at my back—Trinity, the most interesting and I feel like saying the most beautiful. It at least looks more airy than some of them. The cloister around the square facing the river is to be converted to hospitals for the sick and wounded of the war. Soldiers are everywhere here, recruits for Red-Cross and preparations in Pembroke, Downing and Trinity are going on to take care of the wounded. We have been here three days at Mrs. Struggles' (3/6). Accident sent us to her, and it is more pleasant than at a hotel. She has her house filled in the

term with students from Clare College. Each student is required
to have a bed-room and sitting-room. I am occupying Kujo's suite,
he being a brother of the Empress of Japan. Mary E. and Ruth
have Ismay's, the son of the Titanic man. Simplicity itself, and not
even attractive looking. Mrs. Struggles is nice, though, and I just
know she keeps tabs on the "masters." She says she signs a paper
from Clare promising to report things, if they don't "keep their
tens" especially. The life must be very interesting for the boys, but
expensive. I imagine her quarters are as cheap as any and she asks
£15 a term (10 weeks) furnishing nothing. They usually dine at
their college hall. Our breakfasts with her have been excellent (1s)
[one shilling]. Matthew & Son furnishes a fine luncheon (1/6), the
daintiest cakes and breads I ever ate! How we have enjoyed poking
around town! And we are fickle enough to like the college we are
visiting, at that moment, the best.

Five o'clock yesterday afternoon we attended services at King's
Chapel. I can never describe the melting beauty of that choral
singing. They didn't use the organ. The Chapel is a gem. Henry VII
has his insignia in every direction. Late in the afternoon a walk
around the streets when the sky is pale and the buildings with their
turrets, steeples silhouetted in a dark outline—it is like a dream
place. Last evening we "discovered" Jesus College. The colleges in
a line with their backs on the river have so entranced us that we've
never been able to wander elsewhere. The many-toned bells are
ringing the hour—seven—it will not be dark until nine. The English
twilights in summer are so lovely. We got a boat yesterday late, and
I had Ruth's and Mary E's lives in my hands for an hour, a delightful
hour to me, though they sat very stiffly in their seats. The stream is
so quiet, and even the passing boats glide almost noiselessly by. It is
such fun running under the pretty bridges.[17]

Aug. 14, London

Imperial [Hotel]. Everything is really like a dream, especially
when traveling. Was it only yesterday that we went to Ely from
Cambridge and only at four forty this afternoon that we left again
for London? Ely is only sixteen miles from C[ambridge]. The
cathedral is well worth a long journey to see. The mixed periods

of architecture in these Eng. cathedrals stimulate the intelligence
and my imagination. Each transition marks something noteworthy
in England's history too, usually. Only the sad thing is that every
stage of the growth includes a restoration due to a demolishment by
Cromwell or the Protestants after him. The very charming chapels
right and left of the choir at Ely's are bereft of statues in niches. The
stone work, however, is still exquisite and full of fanciful grinning
imps, which are to the casual observer only foliage. Rackham must
have felt the influence and charm of the old stone carvers.[18] The
verger was unusually good—told his story with quaintness and
freshness. The interior aside from the grand and simple style, is
unique in the colored ceilings. The main part of the structure is
Norman. The Galilee Porch they [say] is unexcelled in England.
Certainly it is a beautiful thing. Until the train was nearly ready to
go back we lingered in the cool shelter of the cathedral, leaving it
only for lunch. It took only thirty minutes to be in Cambridge at
4:30 P.M. We got some delicious pure ice cream at Hawkins (near
Struggles 18 Sidney St.) and after a little rest went towards the river
to read and write until dinner. Mrs. Struggles was to provide the
meal (2/6). A most appetizing repast—soup, fish, meat, vegetables,
salad, fresh fruit with cream—and a savory to end! We ate until I
was ashamed. Afterwards Mrs. Struggles came in and we engaged
her in conversation, not a difficult thing to do. Her talk revealed, as
she had before shown, a sweet, wholesome, generous nature, honest
and humble. Very naively she told of her life, ambitions, her lack
of education, her pride in her daughter who had married above
her "platform" as she put it, and the consequent snubs from [her]
husband's family to her. I wish I could have a record of her talk,
thoroughly refreshing.

The next morning we started for Jesus again, to see the chapel
with the Burne-Jones-Morris windows. It is quite a bit annoying the
put-off hours they have. We finally got in, Ruth and I, at half after
eleven, and well worth our while it was to wait. The old verger was
sweet. He told us about each window quite patiently, reveled in their
color and beauty himself which added no doubt to our appreciation.
Madox Brown and someone else finished some of the windows,
quite beautiful, too.[19] Jesus is very like a monastery and the chapel

has large parts belonging to the nunnery dating back somewhere in 1200. The organ used for daily service is 300 years old, black keys for white, and white for black. The old man took us up to see it and asked if we played. Imagine our childish joy—so he pumped and we played "Nearer My God to Thee." Lovely sweet tones came forth with all the stops on. After lunch we visited Christ College, and of course the mulberry tree planted by Milton. The tree was full of luscious ripe berries, tasted quite as good as raspberries. At 4:35 we took the train for London again. They are running quite often and regularly.

Aug. 20, London

Decided to stay at the Imperial where we had checked our things until we could find a pension. Saturday I started forth to that end. Most of the addresses I had were in our vicinity. It was most discouraging—cheap, horrid, messy places—nice people trying to make themselves feel respectable in them. Finally I crossed town and tried around Hyde Park. Such affluence! Found the place where I now am: 9 Porchester Terrace, charming 2 ½ guineas a week, a little higher than some but unlike anything in Russell Sq. part. We feel calmer and restful out here and the inconvenience is nothing to mention.

Monday [August 24] Mary E. and I saw "Great Adventure" at Kingsway Theatre. Arnold Bennett's play perfectly splendid. Tuesday afternoon I wandered in New Bond St., falling into Tooth's art gallery where I had a most pleasant time.[20] The dealer was quite chatty and helped me much with the pictures. Found a print shop on Oxford 405 where anything printed is kept—or nearly—in stock. I ordered my beloved "Parnassus" by Mantegna, 12/s.

At night [Tuesday, August 25] went to my first Promenade Concert at Queen's Hall.[21] Until Part II I was in heaven. Most excellent orchestra. Fine balance and lovely quality, Sir Henry Wood seems a fine conductor. Really I was quite intoxicated with the music. Percy Grainger, a beautiful youth with a halo of golden hair, directed one of his compositions: "Colonial Song," virile and fresh, and an Irish Reel.[22] The audience was extremely enthusiastic. Downstairs is where they stand, crowded. We sat in 2/s. seats which are unreserved. Most of the men in the orchestra looked English—28 first violins & seconds—8 cellos, 6 basses, 8 or ten violas, I forget, a good choir of woods and brasses. The cellos are particularly good. The programmes are being altered on account of the war. All England is putting the ban on German things, and they are carrying it into concerts as well. Very little Beethoven, no German moderns. Mondays they always have a Wagner night—none now—no Strauss and Erich Korngold. However, I hear pressure is being brought to have the programs as usual. Patriotic music begins and ends the programmes. The big pipe organ with full orchestra gives a tremendous effect. Last night, Wednesday [August 26], Brahms 3rd Symphony was magnificently played.

Yesterday I spent the day at the British Museum. In the morning, Ruth and I leisurely enjoyed the Elgin marbles and in the afternoon I was in the students' rooms sitting at a table and revelling in the collection of book-plates. Am having a tailor suit made at Delaroche on Regent Street. 11 ½ guineas. Fiddled and loafed away a pleasant day. Do hope this fine weather lasts. Can wear light weight suits and silk gowns in the day without coats: London looks more cheerful and we are beginning to gather our wits.

London may have been more cheerful, but the war was not going well for England. From August 24 to September 1 the British Expeditionary Forces were in retreat in France, moving toward the Marne River, but fighting continued, and casualties on both the German and Allied sides were heavy.

Aug. 30, London

Horrors heap themselves upon horrors. The war rages. Papers are livid with German atrocities. Someday I hope, the truth will assume its true proportions. I'm sure some of the things have happened. When a nation calls upon all its men, and there is compulsory military service, reason should expect barbarities. War has always awakened the lowest in man. I can recall no war, even our Civil War, where one people fought among themselves, where the offensive side didn't outrage every known good human instinct. One's sympathies are torn in such a conflict, especially when the

beauty and culture of one is as clear as the liberal government—and
what it stands for—of the other. What hurts is that I know that the
Allies in the war will be just as contemptuous of the wonderful
cities in Germany as the Germans have already seemed to be in
Belgium. What a waste of precious things, not alone of lives! I find
the most refined of English desire to see Germany "wiped off the
face of the earth," knowing in their hearts their indebtedness. They
do not mean as a government but as a nation. Little do they realize
that the act of destroying her can not at the same time communicate
her wealth of native talents and qualities.

However, the case against the ruling powers in Germany does
seem convicting. The future will hold truer facts, more truth than
now. And Germany should lose, but I do trust not her identity. The
Promenade Concerts are now giving the Wagner programmes.
Last Monday night was the first, received with storms of approval.
The English are a fair minded people in many ways. And they do
love music, and listen like Germans. The orchestra played well, too.
The prelude to Act I Meistersinger was delightfully played. How
Wagner could write—how he plays with the fugue form in this
overture! Wagner is the master, truly, here. On Wednesday night
[August 26] the Fifth Symphony was played, superb Beethoven.
And Friday night [August 28] his second, and a Bach Cantata "Non
sa che" with a symphony prelude. Mme. Jessie Brett Young sang
the difficult recitative and aria wonderfully and without music
or words[23]—I should say notes. At the concert last Friday Aug.
22 [Aug. 21] Solomon, a child, played Beethoven's First Concerto
superbly, remarkable for tone, technic and abandon.[24] The concerts
are really a treat. They are one among the many things which bind
me to London right now. I have decided that the main reason I love
London is that they have no street cars. The clatter and clang of NY
is missing, and the buses are more convenient. Then the police are
the most efficient, kindly, fatherly persons. As Mrs. Leavell says,
"The police and I are as one." You can always get an answer to any
question.

Lately the National Gallery has been opened. All you have to
do is to register on entering. Every morning from 10:15 to 12:30
with 15 minutes intermission, lectures are given by as delightful

and instructive [a] man as I've ever heard. I could stand until I drop listening. Have heard only the whole of two mornings as yet, Monday on the Umbrians and the Venetians, and Tuesday on the Tuscans. He was so absorbed with his love for the Tuscans Tuesday that he spent all his time on a very few pictures, and glorified da Vinci and Michel Angelo in positive terms. He said that to him of all the works extant in art—painting or sculpture—The Awakening of Man in the Sistine Chapel was the name of sublimity and supreme as a work of art. I hope I am not over-stating it.

Mrs. Leavell and I met Sunday 24th [23rd] in Aldgate again— Petticoat Lane—and mixed with the Jews around their booths. A seething mass, they are trading in the streets. There were few strangers and they were almost unnoticed. I fell to the allurements of a silver goblet claimed to be George III. It is nice. Sunday is the day of days in Petticoat Lane, a sight unique. Mrs. Leavell and I have the antique fever now. It hasn't hurt us as yet. We poke around, but buy little or nothing. Last night a charming shop in Richmond entertained our interest so late that we had to eat out there, getting home [at] 11:30. The trip back [by] <u>33 Bus</u> was beautiful. Today we are going to Hampton Court "on-top-a-bus." Our trip yesterday was delightful. The jolly crowds do not look like they know anything about the war. Just as many young men as women. Of course they do know and care, but I am continually impressed with the idea that the people are apathetic. Everything has posters in red letters appealing for men. The papers are full of it. A great many are, I think, like a man I heard on a bus say, "The war's an awful bother—a nuisance." He was quite young enough and hale enough to have fought for his country. On the other hand if men enough can be found to fight, the very element which wants to grumble at it and stay at home will be able to keep the wheels moving. With the Russians at the east of P[russia] really the English needn't worry.[25] In the end, they'll get whatever they dictate, anyhow. Still, I like these English even if they do make me impatient. We need some of their qualities. I suppose because I love the Germans makes me irritated with them. In Germany I have, though, been just as put out with a certain class there. We have the same at home. I am sure that each country has some predominant characteristics and that human nature deep down remains the same.

Friday 28 Mary E., Ruth, and the McClendons went to Harrogate. Mrs. Leavell remained, I'm glad to say.

Thursday 27th Rowena Teagle,[26] after receiving a note from me, came in her car and took me to their place an hour and a half from L[ondon]. You go through beautiful country along by fine estates. Her place (leased) is what seems typical of the comfortable, elegant country life you imagine. The gardens particularly fascinated me. The vegetables and fruits are as prettily laid out as any flower garden. Flowers are planted here and there among the vegetables, Rowena was so sweet and made me wish I'd let her know sooner. They sailed for N.Y. on Saturday [August 29].

Ima and some of her companions did not leave London until mid-September. In the meantime, they amused themselves by shopping for antiques and listening to political speeches.

Sept. 10

While we are not regularly sight-seeing our days are crowded. I'm afraid we are too ambitious and rest very little. If it weren't for the nights being also busy, busy days wouldn't matter. Several of the good programmes I have deliberately stayed away from [in] the Promenade Concerts. Somehow Mrs. L. and I get interested in whatever we are doing and overdo the things until we have a rush to get back for lunch or dinner as the case may be. The antique fever left me rather the worse for having had the attack. I got a silver tea set, really a dream, and such a bargain I couldn't resist it—persuading myself to do without the dressy winter suit I was planning. We "antiqued" until we got into a silver shop in Church Street, and where I got my tea service was the finishing place. The shop-man was so excited over us—a character—and ready to bargain. Everybody claims the war makes things cheap. He said we didn't know what it meant to him. We told him we knew what it meant to us. Well all three of us got excited, and before I knew it I was ready to buy anything. The next day I was calmer and with clear reason decided on the tea things. Our education is enlarging

on the score of antiques and we've about decided that new things at
good shops are really cheaper. We visited some on Oxford [Street]
and found the clerks just as delighted to show us things and tell
us about them as could be although we'd tell them we were not
possible purchasers. Thursday [September 10] we heard about War
Appeal for recruits, which was to be at Guild Hall near Cheapside.
Asquith, Churchill and many others were to talk, so we determined
to get there by some means.[27] So we went to Guild Hall to inquire if
ladies were permitted at the meeting. At the door a lovely officer—
soldier—gave us his promise to see that we got in.

Friday morning [September 11] an hour before time we found
ourselves in a huge crowd bound for the meeting. There were
almost no women, it looked impossible and police were lined up as
if to prevent people from trying to rush in. We were about to give
up, but Mrs. L.'s heart was set on seeing the whole business. We
therefore edged along until we were not far from the entrance, and
suddenly orders were given by the police to form a line four abreast.
We found ourselves marching into the hall. On passing the soldier
I committed one of the most humiliating acts of my life—offered
him money! He blushed and bowed his refusal! I thought everybody
in Eng. expected a tip, altho my better judgment had told me he
was a gentleman. At any rate it was tipping that got us the beautiful
view to be had from the gallery. Some women were present—but
very few.

Below us the jams of men, the platform at the end of the hall
with the distinguished men, the beautiful hall, brass bands and
the occasion for coming together—composed a memorable event.
The Lord Mayor in his grandeur introduced Asquith. Bonar Law
followed,[28] then Balfour and cries from the men brought a short
talk from Churchill. Asquith talked so indistinctly and with very
little charm or magnetism. His voice rang now and then with a quite
bitter tone, so that with the few phrases I caught, I had thought,
until I afterwards read his speech in the paper, that he had made a
prejudiced talk. On the other hand Bonar Law spoke with frankness
and a firmness which sounded very different from the cold words
in that afternoon's paper. Churchill looked like Mr. Micawber, or
a Dickens demagogue, but nothing impressed us like the police. A

magnificent one in the gallery, the immortal 177, did all he could
to take care of the comfort of the ladies. Mrs. L. offered him a tip,
too, and he bowed his thanks with refusal—two in one day! 177
impressed me too, so much that I told Mrs. Royse, a lady at our
pension, that it was a pity poor King George didn't look as fit as
the policemen, and she looked so pained, I was all regrets.[29] These
people are bound by chains of iron to every silly tradition in the
land, and they bow their heads still to the superiority of the nobility.
I've actually found that the middle class believes in divine right of
the king and will attempt to prove some ridiculous theory of descent
from an Israelite premier who landed in Ireland in the days of
Abraham!

The Church of England goes hand in hand with the state, and
justifies its acts by quoting Scripture from the pulpit on Sunday. At
Westminster Abbey I heard a bishop preach on the war and take
England as the hand of God! Blasphemy, I call it! The idea of mixing
God and Christ in such a war of jealousy and hatred! The bishop
did with good lack of logic say we were living in an unchristian
Christendom, and said we did not deserve the happiness and
comfort of peace. War would continue to exist in a world as wicked
at heart as ours.

We have found the speaking in Hyde Park most illuminating,
and a new point of view as to England's "honor" is dimly
foreshadowed by some statements heard there. Even in these
stirring times, free speech is permitted in this zone. One Sunday
night we listened first to a woman passionately calling for recruits.
All England in fact is wanting and talking recruits. They are great
people to "hear, hear" and cheer and sing patriotic songs, but they
exhaust their enthusiasm in that way and continue going after
their interests—playing cricket and so on. As far as I saw, out of the
immense crowd none of the young men went up to give their names
to the recruiting officer present.

From this meeting we went where things proved both exciting
and surprising. A socialist was condemning the war, and calling
upon the laboring class to stay at home. They had no duty to a
government that in time of peace ignored their interests. Besides,
this was a war deliberately planned. It seems Snowden and other

members of Parliament had made startling exposure of a trust of armaments, gunpowder and dreadnought, which had for its largest stock-holders admirals of the British Navy and men high in state.[30] The White Paper we were told had given only part of the telegrams and "conversations." Before Germany entered Belgium she had as a final advancement to England asked England's neutrality on any grounds Eng. would lay down. Finally the socialist speaker said he was not pro-German, he was not pro-English; his only flag was the red flag of socialism. He called the King a commonplace man who sat in Buckingham Palace while old women starved at his gate! And large crowds cheered him. I was frightened all the time for fear there'd be a riot. During a time like this such views couldn't seem possible to be so popular. Opposing the socialist was speaking a minister of the gospel justifying <u>War</u>. When someone from the audience asked if Christ had ever said anything to show that war was right, Scripture was quoted, and a howl of fury went up from the mob. The other day, I was in a little shop in Charing Cross Road where so many socialistic books were that I asked the old man if he were a socialist. He said "no" he was an anarchist. He became very communicative and raved about or against Christianity and the Church. He did believe in Jesus and a God, but this Christ they were telling him about, he would have none of it. Well—I can't blame him if they are being taught as I have heard them preach since war began. It is blasphemy and wickedness. This last Sunday [September 13] we went into the park again to hear our socialist. War is growing more popular. The crowd was part hissing and part cheering—immense crowd. The cross questions became so noisy and the mob so violent, the police came to escort the speaker out of the park. But he had to have his last say. If he were speaking for the government, the police would have quieted the crowd, but now they would make him stop talking. They in fact pulled him down and I suppose he was locked up for two months for disturbing the peace. At least when I asked one of [the] regular socialist speakers what they'd do to him, they said he'd be locked up. It was a dreadful experience. Mrs. L. and I had to rush against the fence to keep from being crushed by the crowd.

One day Miss Royse, the dear little English lady, took us—

Mrs. L. and me—to St. Thomas's hospital to visit the wounded
soldiers. There were many there. We carried them baskets of fruit
and flowers, altho we didn't expect to go into the wards. The nurses
insisted on our going. Most of them were away from home and
friends and were well enough to talk. And we found them glad to
talk. The last two we spoke with had been in the battles of Mons
and Namur.[31] They said the Germans were being killed, just as
the papers said, in shocking numbers. The officers got behind the
Germans with a pistol and drove them ahead. One little fellow
who told us so much said he'd be awfully glad to get back. "It was
more sport than anything." He spoke so enthusiastically about the
English officers. Often in battle a word of encouragement from an
officer would put new life into the soldiers. He said their officers led
their men—right in the front. One thing I didn't quite understand
was how he knew about the German officers, because he told me
also that they never got nearer the enemy than three hundred
yards, and that for the smoke they couldn't see each other. They
fired without direct aiming. He said the Germans were not good
gun shots too, which also seemed inconsistent. One thing is sure—
the loss of life among the Germans has been fearful. The recruits
practice every day in Kensington, really at our very door. We passed
them every morning going down by bus. People gather about to
watch, so we joined the throng one morning. The audience proved
to be French, Spanish, Belgian, all nationalities. This morning it
was drizzling, so we kept under umbrellas and formed into knots
quite near the soldiers. It is a most informal gathering. The soldiers
lie down to rest and the officer talks to them in such a nice friendly
way. Then they get up and practice. We were there for the mode of
attack. The company breaks up into little squads, and seem to form
an odd figure in a scattered sort of way. They advance crouching as
near [to the] ground as possible running only a little distance at a
time, then at command drop suddenly flat, all together if possible.
That seemed to be the thing to accomplish—get up and fall down,
all at once—which kept one from getting hit for a target.

 This wonderful park. What do they not use it for? All the pretty
little tots run about at will, the anarchists harangue the multitude,
the recruits practice and the loafers live here. And loafers they

are, countless hundreds stretched out like drugged beings. Lovers meet and walk and do not disguise their affection. I used to think Germany rather immodest in this respect, but Hyde Park can hold its own anywhere.

One of our favorite haunts is Charing Cross Road between Oxford St. and Trafalgar. On a rainy day nothing is more fascinating than browsing in the old book shops. Mrs. Leavell has bought all the biographies of all her broken down heroes, at a song, too. Any book on Byron or Napoleon or Wilde, or any of the crown[ed] heads she falls upon with avidity. I think 177 deserves a little hall of Fame![32] We paddled one rainy day until too late for dinner. We had something to eat at a queer place, and then went to see "My Lady's Dress" by [Arthur] Knobloch. Our arms were full of books and socialist literature. The ensemble was complete. "My Lady's Dress" is really fine. An idea changed but akin to Wilde's "Young King." The "Silver King" by Arthur Jones, an old melodrama revived, was worth seeing, and "Bluff King Hal" by [Louis N.] Parker. Theatres are always crowded.

At the end of that fateful summer, in mid-September, Ima Hogg was at last able to book passage on a ship home. She had sailed from Galveston on the *Chemnitz* on July 11.

Left London Sept. 15 for Liverpool sailing 16th on N.Y. American Line for N.Y. Mrs. Leavell and Mr. Thorpe put us into the crowded train and my bags went into the van. At L[iverpool] without claim checks—so it is in Eng. I ran up and down the platform from coach to coach hunting in vain for my fourth piece of luggage! It never turned up. I then went to the lost department at the station, and they wired around the country until the bag was located. The next day it arrived and was put on the ship. How it ever got found after taking the tour up Manchester way is a mystery to me. After all these years that they should be content with that hap-hazard system gets me.

On the train in the same compartment were some people just out of Brussels. The American consul got them and some English through the German lines. The lady had been in B[elgium] since

Aug 2nd—couldn't get out—could get no money. She told frightful
tales of German cruelty, people she had met whose families had
met with murder and cutting. In B[russels] all was well except for
occasional looting. The young man said Belgium had been on the
verge of a revolution—suffrage and labor troubles. In the same
compartment were two Irish ladies who talked about the troubles
there. It seems though the papers say nothing, Ireland has not
forgotten. These ladies said, no matter which side now, bloodshed
was sure to be the result. And Asquith is pushing Home Rule now.
The Catholic priests, so they tell, have sold to the Nationalists
everything in Ireland by lottery tickets—to be good when Ireland
gets Home Rule. Of course the majority are for the Irish rule—are
Catholics. In the best part of Ireland at least, the most fertile are
at the same time the poor of Ireland. Priest ridden? They say they
are, and lazy. The whole world seems in ferment. Why should we
yet dream of peace as a reality when there is not an establishment
of any sort of justice or equality. Wrath of man against man is
still in men's hearts. It is bound to break out in savage bloodshed.
I do hope it is not necessary yet to take the biological view of the
struggle of nations and mankind that Bernhardi does in his book
on "Germany and the Next War."[33] That book has given me much
food for thought and strange to say, a sympathy for the German
government I did not have before. It has an aim, an ideal, which
it sincerely desires to attain for the nation's sake. First of all she
wants expansion, not unnaturally, for the sake of concentrating
her vitality. Why should her surplus energy expend itself in other
countries? Why should she not make use of that blood in spreading
her ideals, not of government, but of achievement and of thought.
Now that England has satiated herself in the glory of conquest it
is all very well to frown on Germany. France has had her day—it
is past. Russia is murmuring in her sleep, and we in America are
self sufficient, at least—so I hope. The great regret should be that
in our day force of arms should still exist. But it is with us, and
[has] been used quite lately by most every nation in some more or
less minor war. Deep in the nature of Germany there is something
elemental: In time of peace, the creative vitality, in time of war,
cruelty and barbarity. With desperate purpose she has roused all

that is desperate in her blood. The Germans are thorough and intense and intense and sincere. So England is fighting to retain her power and not for "her honor." She has never yet overlooked the dangers of a growing power and with all the keenness of her English diplomacy has crushed each menacing rival down through history. It is not yet time to say whether Germany did indeed give the word for the outbreak of hostilities. Many things point both ways. Of course, any way you look at it the network of international diplomacy has been spun during the past decade so that relations have been strained and unnatural. If Germany was the one to bring it at this moment, she did but the wise thing—as every nation had difficulties of the greatest kind at home—and knowing the spirit existing against her in Europe—as a mere matter of protection—aside from any desire to expand—this was the hour to strike Russia. I do not think she dreamed that England would be able to enter into hostilities. The root of the thing has been the fear of Slav encroachment through Austria and Servia. Germany's geographical place is very unfortunate for a progressive country. So in any case, offensive or defensive, Germany at this time is justified in my opinion. No one—not even she [Germany]—dreamed it would turn into the world war it has—not at this time. When she falls, England will claim the glory. And if it weren't for her colonies she wouldn't have had enough men to engage in a real live campaign. With all England's democratic government she hasn't succeeded in giving the same self-respect and decency to her working classes that Germany has. They wouldn't live in Germany in the midst of such squalor and degradation! With all Germany's military we have a great deal to learn from her. As a paternal government she is superb. Twenty-five years from now we'll see some things which will make us sorry in America that we jumped at our conclusions so quickly.

"Twenty-five years from now," Ima Hogg wrote in September 1914. On September 1, 1939, World War II began.

This is going to be the end of my diary. I have left out so very much which would have been worth my noting. But the strain and excitement of these epoch making days in the beginning told too greatly on my mind. Besides we were in a fever of inquiry, running about trying to realize the situation and in a state of bewilderment wondering what to do. Such a war stuns one. The overwhelming sense of horror at first was the paralyzing thing. The nights as well as the days were full after we settled a little, and so much time elapsed between the writing that everything has been skimmed. I would like to have made this interesting to myself in after years. In Bremen it was my idea when I bought this dear little book, and I tried to make a mental note of each solemn scene so that I should put it down. But the events followed one after another too rapidly and with too much force.

Ima Hogg had conflicted feelings about the Great War. Composing these last two pages, she tore out one and began anew.

It has been a wonderful experience. I am glad I could have seen as much as I have. I really am very grateful for the shelter and hospitality of the world's greatest and in many ways most admirable city—London. She has opened her arms to everyone like a big mother. And they have rushed to her for protection. London has much the same charm that Mrs. Wiggs has,[34] and in my heart I love her and her people!

On September 16, 1914, Ima Hogg sailed from Liverpool aboard the SS *New York*. The McClendon family were fellow passengers, and Ima shared a stateroom with their four-year-old daughter, Elizabeth.[35] They arrived in New York on September 24. By October, Ima was back home in Houston. When the United States entered World War I in 1917, Ima's brother Mike was one of some two hundred thousand American soldiers who took part in the last battles.[36]

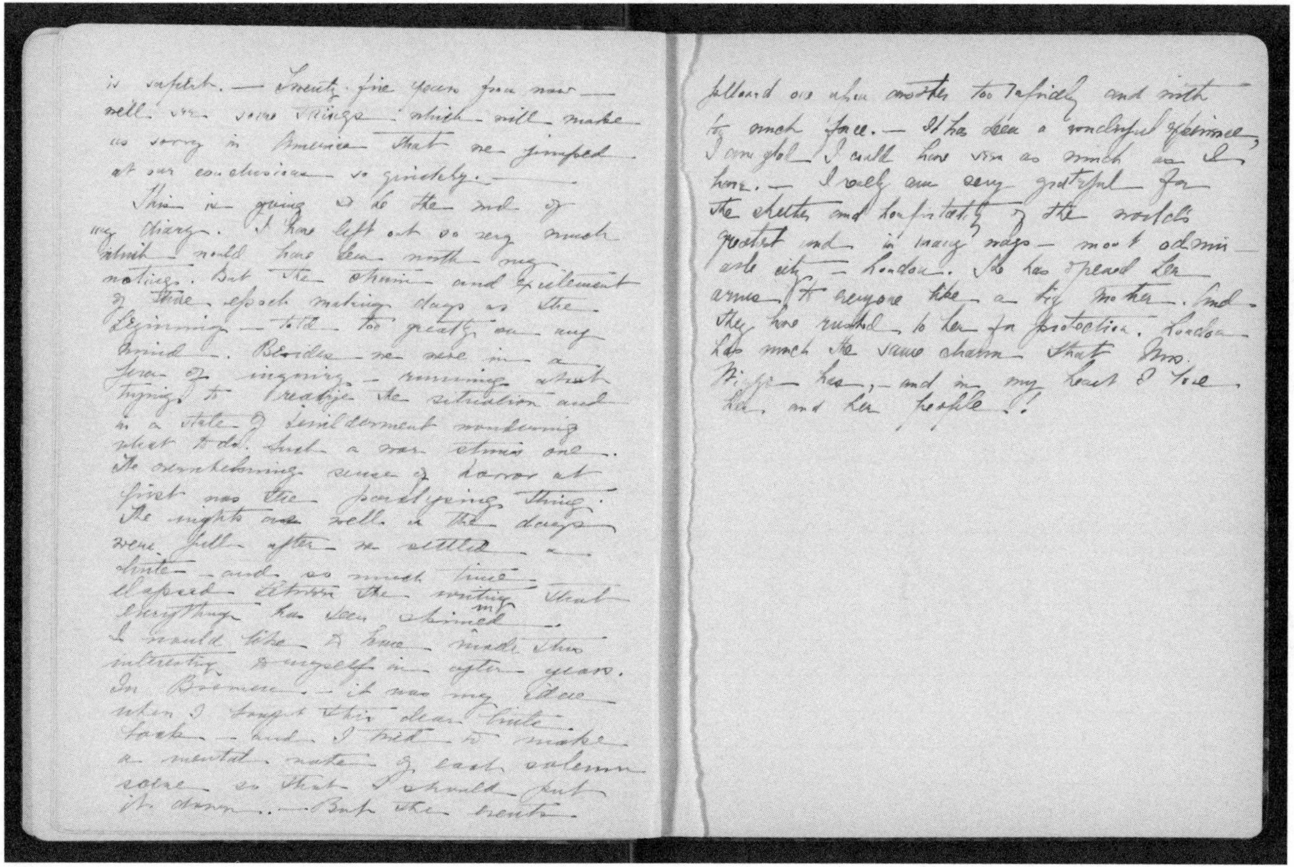

Figure 10. 1914 diary, one page torn out

5

The 1918 Notebook

A Mystery

By 1918 the war that had begun in 1914 had turned into a bloody stale-mate. Battle trenches stretched like a jagged wound across the map of Europe from the North Sea to the border of Switzerland. In 1917 the United States had declared war on Germany, and in 1918 US troops joined the Allied Forces battling German troops. Ima Hogg, pro-German at the war's beginning, now had divided loyalties: Her brother Mike was Captain Mike Hogg of 90th US Infantry Division, 180th Brigade, 360th Regiment, Company D, 1st Battalion. He sailed for France on June 14, 1918, and fought on the Western Front from August 21 until the cease-fire of November 11.

On the home front, the Houston Symphony felt the war: A number of musicians had enlisted and shipped out for "Over There." That forced the young and struggling Houston Symphony, which Ima had helped found in 1913, to cancel its 1918–19 season. Ima, who had been unanimously elected as the symphony's president in May, felt the loss most keenly.[1]

As the summer of 1918 began, Ima hoped to forget her worries as she set off on a vacation trip to Lake Placid, New York, and other points east. Her travel companion was a close friend, Estelle Sharp, the widow of a prominent Houston oilman. Estelle was forty-five; Ima, thirty-six.

The two had worked together on the Houston Symphony and moved in the same social circles. Now they would escape Houston's summer heat, spending time at an exclusive resort.[2] Ima also planned a drive through New York, Pennsylvania, and parts of New England to shop for antiques and to do research on other symphony orchestras. At the beginning of the trip she bought a small spiral notebook, the kind that stenographers used. What she wrote—and did not write—in it adds to the store of secrets she kept.

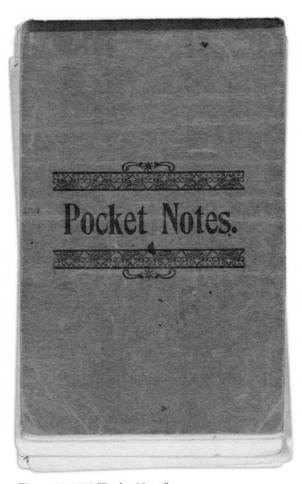

Figure 11. 1918 "Pocket Notes"

She wrote on the first page: "Summer" and on the next line, "1918."
This was not to be a diary. Ima did not need to record travels in New
York and New England, where she had vacationed many times. This
notebook was to be, as the name on its cover promised, "Pocket Notes"
for random jottings: addresses of antiques dealers, items purchased, and
statistics about symphony orchestras in other cities. Although Ima had
lists of topics, such as "Orchestra population, Auditorium attendance,"
that she wanted to investigate, that research remained undone. The
notebook has no facts about any other symphony orchestras. It contains
no dates, and its random entries fill thirty-six pages.[3] Toward the end,
the notebook changes: Some pages are crossed out with a large X. Ragged
edges between others show a page or pages torn out. Some entries are
upside down or out of order, as if written in haste, without looking to
see if the diary was right side up. The content of the pages changes from
notes about orchestra sizes and budgets and lists of antiques purchased,
to copies of poems about war and death in battle. Something unforeseen
happened to Ima Hogg that summer.

Her vacation trip began on a hopeful note. On the first page, after the
date, Ima jotted down addresses of antiques dealers and items to look at.

> **Mrs. E. La Ferriere**
> **146 N. Main**
> **Mechanicville, N.Y.**
>   **oxen wagon double chairs**
> **Springfield Economy Rug Co.**
> **17 Taylor St. Springfield**
> **(Thomas Mailiff)**
> **Alice Brown— Shelburne Falls Mass.**[4]

Always careful with her money, she recorded every purchase, including the candy she bought: "Pecan hearts .85 Butternuts 1.00." The entries
in this notebook reveal that Ima Hogg had a keen interest in acquiring
antiques before she became known as a discerning collector of early
American art and furniture. She once said, "Collecting is a disease. I
think I had it from childhood."[5] In the summer of 1918 she was collecting
again, evidently planning to furnish a house with treasures she found

on her travels. Her notebook contains a rough sketch of a floor plan, the first floor of a two-story structure.[6] It was probably the house at 4410 Rossmoyne, which she shared with her brothers Will and Mike. Tom, the youngest brother, was married and living in Colorado. Will was making some improvements on this rental property and planning to buy it, which he would do in 1919. Ima was shopping for antiques, most likely for the refurbished house.

This second page, as are all the other pages in this notebook, is un-dated.

Clock 13.00 B. 4.00
Beds 20.00 Poudre 2.34
Benj. H. Lindes, Lake George, NY.
R D. 2
Nichols & Stone Co. (chairs paid)
82 Logan Mass.
Brooklyn Chair Co.
425-433 W. 28th St. N. J. [N.Y.]
Mrs. Hubbell 45 ½ Park St.
Mrs. Spooner Glenn [Glens] Falls, N.J., [N.Y.]
Quilts

As the summer of 1918 began, perhaps after her stay at the Lake Placid resort, Ima was on the hunt for antiques in New York and New England. She apparently purchased chairs from Nichols & Stone, a famous fur-niture manufacturer in Gardner, Massachusetts. The Brooklyn Chair Company was advertising antique chairs in 1918. Mrs. Spooner of Glens Falls, New York, dealt in quilts as well as a wide range of other antiques.[7]

In that fateful summer of 1918 Captain Mike Hogg was also on the move, on the way to the Western Front. In early June he wrote to Ima: "Passed right through New York. . . . Will write you every week over there." After the Battle of Saint-Mihiel in September he wrote to Ima: "Except for this month, you have received at least one letter a week from me. That is, I have written that many."[8]

On June 14 Captain Hogg sailed for France and wrote to Ima from aboard ship on June 15, saying that all was well. "I have seen no one who is a bit uneasy about U-Boats. . . . I wish there were more I could tell you, but it can't be done."[9] Military censorship forbade such news. All he could send to her was this letter:

> Military Post Office, Soldiers' Mail
> The ship on which I sailed has arrived safely overseas.
>   Mike Hogg
>   American Expeditionary Force

That would have been sometime after June 21, when Mike was again on land and on his way to France. He wrote to Ima from France on June 23, describing the pleasant weather and the charms of French children. He ended the letter with "I don't know when you will get this."[10] Military mail was always uncertain. Mike did not know when he would receive mail from home, either. On July 8 Mike wrote to Ima: "We have received no mail so far. I have an idea that you are up in New Hampshire again this summer. No reason to have such an idea, but you liked it so much before that I thought you would 'head' that way." At the end of the letter, Mike wrote, "I hope you and the other members of the family are as well as I am."[11]

A letter from Mike to Ima on August 7, 1918, complains that he has written to her every week, but he has not heard from her lately. Another letter on September 3 wonders if she is receiving his weekly letters. Mike did not know that his sister had been taken ill in July.

On July 11 (one day after Ima's thirty-sixth birthday) Will Hogg received a telegram from Dr. Gavin Hamilton, a Houston physician and family friend. He told Will that Ima was "suffering from a marked degree of anaemia" and was "much run down, . . . particularly her nerves." Dr. Hamilton evidently had heard this from Ima's traveling companions. Helen Thompson, who had known Ima since their 1907 European tour, had joined Estelle Sharp to travel with Ima. They were concerned enough about her to consult Dr. Hamilton.[12] Was Ima's condition brought on by something that happened in June?

From June 1 to June 26, the Battle of Belleau Wood raged on and on. Day after day, newspaper headlines in large type reported Germany's devastating losses. Ima could not have avoided them. On June 9, for example, the *New York Times* banner front-page headline read: "Germans

Gain 2 ½ Miles, Loss of Men Appalling. Battle Described as Fiercest of the War." The news from the front grew worse for Germany day by day, until the American victory on June 26.

It is not beyond the realm of possibility that Ima received a letter or cablegram with news of the death in battle of someone she loved. Her brother Mike was not yet in combat. The one she mourned may have been a German.[13] If so, Ima kept it to herself, but the toll it took on her health was obvious.

At Will's urging, Ima cut short her travels in Pennsylvania and New England and returned to New York City, accompanied by Estelle Sharp and Helen Thompson. On July 20 Will consulted with them about "drs. for Miss Ima." On July 21 Will took Ima for a drive, but she suffered from "nausea." On July 29 Will received a letter from a Houston friend, Edward Prather, who repeated Dr. Hamilton's concerns about Ima:

> Dr. Hamilton thinks that Ima is in a very serious condition and that most anything could happen unless she goes and gets a good doctor and is put in bed and kept quiet for several weeks. He told us that he had wired you. . . . Mrs. Thompson called Mrs. Prather yesterday and told her that Ima has positively refused to go to a sanitarium. . . .[14]

Ima, always independent, was difficult to persuade. Will took her to dinner in New York on August 1, with an outcome unrecorded. More that a week later, on August 9, Will and Estelle Sharp journeyed to Lake Placid "to look up camp for Miss Ima & Mrs. Sharp." That trip was unsuccessful. At last, on August 13, Will wrote in his diary that Ima and Estelle Sharp had left "for camp in Maine." They were bound for "Spinny's Camp," as Will called it, in Rockwood, a remote, rustic campsite on the northwest shore of Moosehead Lake.[15] They stayed there until sometime in September.

Meanwhile, Ima's brother Mike saw action in France on August 22 and fought in the Battle of St. Mihiel, which ended September 15. He wrote to Ima on September 23: "I have received a great many letters from you." Those letters have not been located. Ima and Mike were only three years apart in age, and she was closer to him than to Will or Tom. She had toured Europe with Mike, a trip that included twelve days in Berlin, which Ima had left blank in her 1910 travel diary. Mike would have known whom they saw and what they did in Berlin, where Ima had lived for nearly a year. Now he was in Germany, fighting Germans.

In the summer of 1918, Ima was fighting another kind of battle. "Roughing it" in the Maine woods was not improving her condition. Will Hogg consulted with specialists in New York City and decided to move Ima to a renowned sanitarium in Kerhonkson, New York. Its founder, Dr. Andrew Green Foord, advertised the scenic site on the slope of the Shawangunk Mountains, which afforded a "wonderful view," where "[e]xcellent water, skilled assistants, and absolute quiet make 'Nonkanawha'—i.e. by the side of the stream—a mecca for overworked people. . . ."[16] Ima agreed to try it. Evidently it suited her; she stayed there from October 1 to December 4.

She kept her little notebook, and she read. She made notes on what she read, as the following passages on page 3 from an October 19, 1918, magazine article show. The next three pages consist of Ima's notes on an article she read in the *Dial*, a journal of literary and political essays.[17] It was not light reading.

> **Oct. 19 Dial**
> **Reconstructing Am. Bus.**
> **Ante bellum 25 billion per mun.[?]**
> **Nor. orders [?] 46 billion**
> **18,000,000 people changed occupations.**
> **What gov. action would business like?**
> **. . .**
> **Industrial Councils in Eng.**

Page 4 contains more reading notes on "Industrial wealth." Page 5 continues the reading notes.

> **Aim at industrial, economic liberty, enlarging opportunities of workers. . . .**
>   **If N.Y. can subscribe a billion dollars at a time for a Liberty Loan, it can be taxed a billion for a Humanity Loan.**
>   **Will then be changes in the individual psychology of man's and woman's outlook upon the most intimate and sacred problems of life.**

Here it looks as if page 6 was neatly cut off. Page 7 is blank except for
one unidentified passage.

> If the people are to hold the key to power, if they would rule they
> must serve, and if they would be the heirs of time they must begin
> to think in terms of eternity.

The next few pages, undated, are notes Ima made on research she planned
to do on symphony orchestras in other cities besides Houston. It is not
clear when she wrote these.

[Page 8]

> Orchestra Population: white
> Wealth:
> Philanthropic expenditures
> Citizens in labor & industry:
> Liberty Loan:
> Amusement Exp:
> Auditorium attendance:
> Municipal position on board.
> Co-operation or subsidy for b. & o.?
> How many band instruments available
> Salaries of band men?
> Uses of band?
> [Uses of] orchestra?
> Highest exp. in U.S. for music? (or.)
> city of 150,000?
> Orchestra attendance per capita—
> various cities:

[Page 9]

> Chamber of Commerce relationship various cities—
> Organization of orchestra:
> How many men?
> Day or night?
> How financed?

Average pay by rehearsals
[Average pay by] salary
per week?
Industrial workers as musicians?
How used in other cities?
Conductor:
Community singing
Lecturer
Orchestra conductor?
Band master

[Page 10]

Oratorio conductor:
Salary—
City & orchestra organizations?
Sunday concerts
orchestra—band
Home Talent
Visiting Lecturers
City appropriations for Sunday entertainment
Expense of orchestra
Receipts expected from performances, subscriptions
Deficit proportionate to attendance?

Here a page or pages appear to have been torn out. Then suddenly Ima copied into the notebook on page 11 part of Robert Browning's 1841 verse drama, *Pippa Passes*, describing a sunrise.

Day!
Fast and more fast
O'er night's brim, day boils at last
Boils, pure gold, o'er the cloud cap's brim,
Where spurting and suppress'd it lay—
For not a froth-flake touched the rim
Of yonder gap in the solid gray
Of the eastern cloud, an hour away;

But forth one wavelet, then another, curled,
Till the whole sunrise, not to be supprest,
Rose, reddened, and its seething breast
Flickered in bounds, grew gold, then overflowed the world.
    from Pippa Passes Introduction

Page 12 is a large, hurried scrawl about a possible furniture purchase.

9 chairs Rush
   with new
   Bottoms of Flag
      at 10 Each
      Crated Read[y]
      to Shipp [ship] at
   And clock
   case at 10.00
   with hands—

After this, there appears to be a page or pages torn out. Page 13 is a reading list, obviously out of sequence in this 1918 notebook, since the titles range from the early 1900s to 1920. But for much of 1919 and 1920, Ima was ill and had plenty of time for reading. Ima was a voracious, judicious, intelligent reader. Her tastes were wide ranging: She read novels, plays, and books on political and social issues.

"Outland" Mary Austin
"Iron City" M. H. Hedges
"Marie Grubbe" Jens P. Jacobsen
"The Prestons" Mary H. Vorse
"Americanized Socialism" James MacKaye
"The Education of Henry Adams"
"John Ferguson" St. J. Ervine
"Maureen" Patrick MacGill
"The Foolish Lovers" St. J. Ervine
"The Wind Between the Worlds" Alice Brown
"Lilith" Romaine Rolland
"Woman" Mag. Marx

"Book of Susan" Lee Wilson Dodd
"Letters of A. Chekhov to His Family and Friends"
"Enslaved," John Masefield
"Bertha Garlan" Arthur Schnitzler

These reading choices, mostly novels, are an interesting mix of social commentary, antiwar sentiments, and, perhaps significantly, love stories with strong female heroines.

Outland (1910), by Mary Austin, is a utopian novel, sometimes called a socialist tract, about obsessive love and betrayal with a happy ending.

Iron City (1919) is a novel by M. H. Hedges about industrialization in Beloit, Wisconsin, the women's movement, and labor struggles.

Marie Grubbe: A Lady of the Seventeenth Century (1917), by Jens P. Jacobsen, is based on the life of a Danish noblewoman who becomes the wife of a ferryman.

The Prestons (1918), by Mary H. Vorse, is a humorous novel about an ordinary American family.

James H. MacKaye, *Americanized Socialism: A Yankee View of Capitalism* (1918), was the author of several books on economics, politics, and philosophy.

Henry Adams's now-classic autobiography was just out in 1918.

St. J. [St. John] Ervine was an Irish playwright. His *John Ferguson* is a 1915 melodrama, set in the 1880s, about a family in rural Ulster, Northern Ireland.

Maureen, by Patrick MacGill, is a 1920 novel about Ireland and Sinn Fein, with a tragic heroine.

The Foolish Lovers, also by St. John Ervine, is an Irish love story.

The Wind between the Worlds is a 1920 novel by Alice Brown about a mother who tries spiritualism to communicate with a son lost in the war.

Lilith (1920) is an antiwar play by Romaine Rolland.

The article in *Woman* magazine is about Jenny Marx, wife of Karl. This was probably from the *Independent Woman,* a magazine published by the National Federation of Business and Professional Women's Clubs (New York, 1920–56).

Book of Susan, a 1920 novel by Lee Wilson Dodd, is about a young orphan girl brought up by a wealthy benefactor in the early 1900s.

Letters of A. Chekhov to His Family and Friends (1920) was translated by Constance Garnett.

Enslaved (1920), by John Masefield, is a long poem based on two stories of young lovers.

Bertha Garlan (1914), by Arthur Schnitzler, is the story of a young piano teacher who travels to Vienna and has an affair with a great violinist.

At some time in 1918 or after, Ima continued her furniture shopping, but this page and the next four pages have a large X across them.

Mrs. E. M.—[page corner torn off]	
Broadway—	
Two cushions—	20
One Cherry tip table—	35
One tip Fyffe table	<u>35.</u>
	82.
[the total 82 has been written over]	87.
1 Trunk	12.00
1 Trunk	15.00
Wagon chair	15.00
2 Prints	8.00
2 Prints	4.00
<u>1 Oxen wagon seat</u>	<u>15.00</u>
	69.
15.	
2.50	
<u>6.00</u>	
23.50	
Mirs.	46.70
66.38	
<u>23.50</u>	23.50
42.85—I owe	
<u>3.00</u>	
39.85—I owe [this line item is crossed out]	
49.85—I owe	305.30

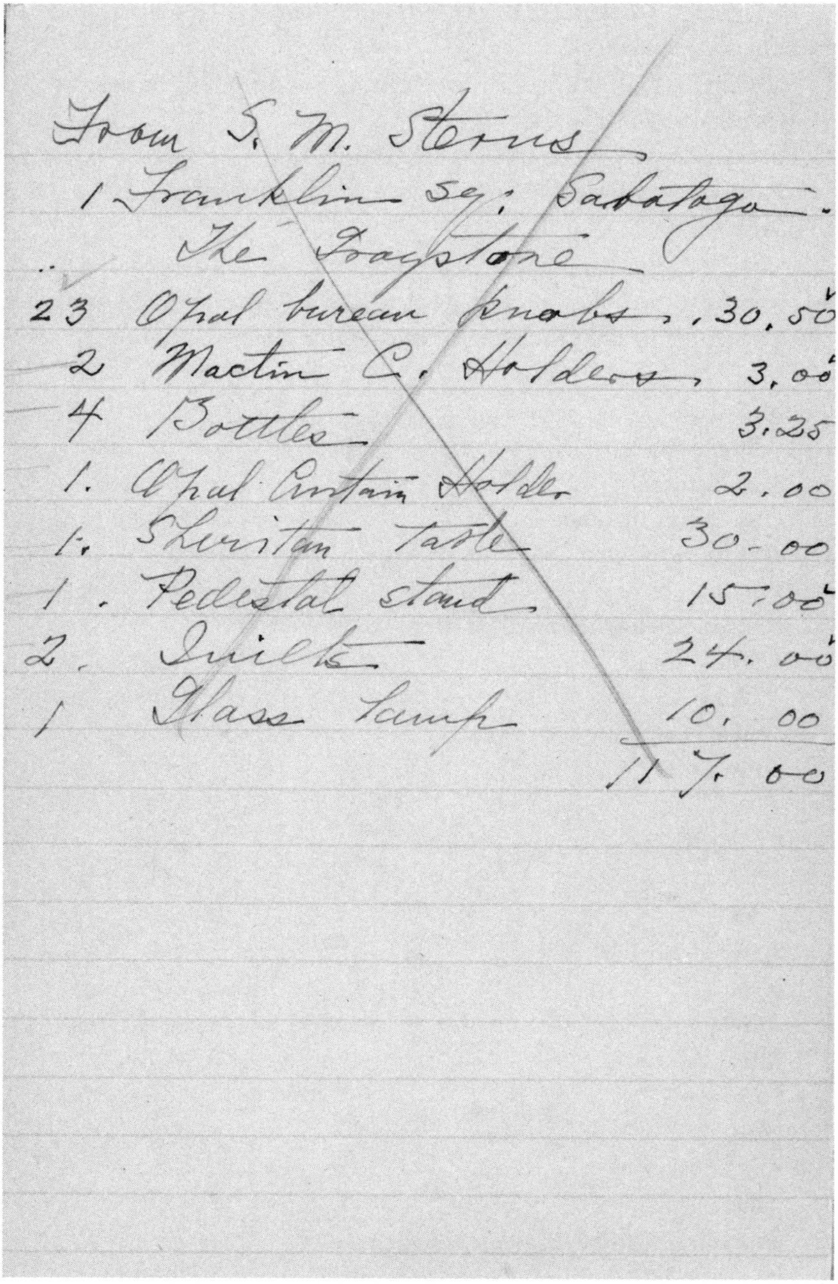

From S. M. Sterns
1 Franklin sq; Saratoga.
The Foagstone

23 Opal bureau knobs, 30, 50
2 Mactin C. Holders, 3, 00
4 Bottles 3.25
1. Opal Curtain Holder 2.00
1. Sheritan Table 30.00
1. Pedestal stand 15.00
2. Quilts 24.00
1 Glass Lamp 10.00
117.00

Figure 12. Sample of 1918 crossed-out page

At the bottom of page 14 are two sets of tally marks adding up to 10.
Page 15 has a large X across it.

Chas. Sherman 145 Bay St.

Racing Picture—	12.00
Two Godey round frames—	10.00
Small Mirror—	15.00
Small Col. [Mirror?]—	12.00
House zinc [?] [Mirror?]—	30.00
Rum bottle—	3.00
Table (dutch)—	25.00
Hook Rugs—	22.00
Mah. Mirror—	25.00
Baby chair—	6.00
Print Cork Harbour—	6.00
Temperance Picture—	8.00
2 Boxes—	5.00
1 Spanish Box	3.00+
Chintz—	10.00
[Chintz]	<u>3.00</u>
195.00	
Leather picture	<u>12.00</u>
	207.00

Red Bottles & Tray	10.00

Page 16 has a large X across it.

Green Bottle (T.)	10.00+
Washington Family	10.00+
3 pieces material	12.00
Portrait	12.00
Wax Flowers	25.00
1 Cherry chest	55.00
Hall [cherry] clock	110.00
Secretary cherry	180.00

Cherry Rocker	22.00
Washstand	<u>10.00</u>
377.00	

Page 17 has a large X across it.

$222.50

Saratoga Sp.	12 Farrington
	L.B. 12 Church St.

Saratoga view—	2.50
Christ at the well—	1.50
Match Box	1.00
Glass Dish (matches)	2.00
Flat Dish (combs & brush)	2.50
4 Dolls—	10.00
Cross Stitch Chair	25.00
l Mah. table (card)	100.00
2 Looking Glasses	24.00
1 China compot.	3.00
Pepper & Salt.	2.00
1 [illegible] Dowd.	<u>1.00</u>
62	174.50
l Lamp	9.00
1 [Lamp]	12.00
1 Spread	10.00
1 [Spread]	9.00
1 Chair (birch)	5.00
1 Sampler	<u>3.00</u>
48.00	

Page 18 has a large X across it.

From S. M. Stearns
1 Franklin Sq. Saratoga
   The Graystone

23 Opal bureau knobs	30.50
2 Mactin C. Holders	3.00
4 Bottles	3.25
1 Opal Curtain Holder	2.00
1 Sheraton Table	30.00
1 Pedestal Stand	15.00
2 Quilts	24.00
1 Glass Lamp	<u>10.00</u>
117.00	

Why were the previous pages crossed out? What became of the items listed as purchased? Page 19 is written on a page with the notebook turned upside down. It is an excerpt from *Journal of a Recluse*, a 1909 novel by Mary Fisher.[18]

> It isn't in the churches that I feel those flights of gratitude and
> an inspiration toward a more complete and noble life, or that
> wonderful interior calm so near to ecstasy, as an excuse to keep the
> soul on earth, and all the coarseness in our life, all our baseness
> shifts from our shoulders like Christian's burden, and rise new
> born to innocent joys, as if the best of childhood had recommenced
> within us. I believe that this feeling of inner purification is the
> essence of what we call religion, and it is also the essence of poetry.
> It is an exaltation which comes from the contemplation of beauty
> and perfection. That is why men who have been very far from
> perfect themselves but who have had a sensitive temperament have
> frequently felt it. Journal of a Recluse

Here some pages appear to have been torn out, and the notebook reverses to its former order, with more symphony research notes.

[Page 20]

> Bl. no. 4196
> How many home musicians of first class for orchestra
> for evening concerts
> Afternoon concerts:
> By rehearsal:
> By salary:
> Chamber of Commerce.
> Band.
> Conductor
> Concerts
> Conductor
> More orchestras
>> 10,000
>> Majestic orchestra
>> Hale
> Letter to Majestic

[Page 21]

> 2014 McKinney
> Musgrove
> Maison Helene—Esplanade Ave.

Page 22 is blank. The notebook is again turned upside down so that pages are reversed. On this page and two other pages are parts of "The Fool," a World War I poem by Robert W. Service, whose brother was killed in that war.[19] What suddenly moved Ima to copy out this tragic poem about a young soldier who died on the battlefield? This is the first of a series of war poems copied into this notebook. She copied "The Fool," perhaps just carelessly, on nonconsecutive notebook pages.

[Page 23]

> The Fool . . . Service
> "But it isn't playing the game," he said—
> And he slammed his books away.

"The Latin & Greek I've got in my head
Will do for a duller day."
"Rubbish!" I cried,
    "The bugle's call
Isn't for lads from school."
D'ye think he'd listen?
Oh not at all:
So I called him a fool, a fool.
Now there's his dog, by
    his empty bed.
And the flute he used to play.
And his favorite bat—
But Dick he's dead—
Somewhere in France
    they say

[Back of Page 23]

Unless the war is rationalized—, spiritualized—harmonized with
the new spirit struggling to be born, all who die, die in vain.
    To-day the increasing close integration of the world which makes
wars utterly destructive makes a world peace conceivable—A sense
of likeness of aim and destiny.[20]

Page 24 continues the poem "The Fool."

Dick, with his rapture of song and sun,
Dick of the yellow hair,
Dicky whose life had just begun
Carrion-cold out there.
Look at his prizes all in a row:
Surely a hint of fame.
Now he's finished with nothing to show.
Doesn't it seem a shame?
Look from the window! All you see
Was to be his one day:
Forest and furrow, lawn and lea,
And he goes and chucks it away.

[Page 25]

> Chucks it away to die in the dark:
> Somebody saw him fall,
> Part of him mud and part of him blood.
> The rest of him—not at all.
> And yet he was never afraid,
> And he went as the best of 'em go;
> For his hand was clenched on his broken blade
> And his face was turned to the foe.
> And I called him a fool!
> Ah, blind was I!
> And the cup of my grief's abrim
> Will glory of England ever

Here some pages appear to have been torn out.

[Page 26]

> die—. . .
> So long as we've fond and fearless fools
> Who, spurning fortune and fame
> Turn out with the rallying
>   cry of the schools—
> Just bent on playing the game.
> A fool! Ah, no! He was more than wise.
> His was the proudest heart.
> He died with the glory of faith in his eyes
> And the glory of love in his heart.
> Though there's never a grave to tell,
> Nor a cross to mark his fall,
> Thank God we know that he "batted well"
> In the last great Game of all.[21]

Page 26 consists of pencil sketches of a house, very likely the house at 4410 Rossmoyne. There is a drawing of the first-floor plan, with a library outlined heavily, and a drawing of the outside of the house from a side view, with a large chimney. Page 27 contains a note and a quotation from George Bernard Shaw.

> Bernard Shaw in a letter to Pearson's Magazine said: "I am ready
> to admit that after contemplating the world and human nature
> for nearly sixty years, I see no way out of the world's misery, but
> the way which would have been found by Christ's will if he had
> undertaken the work of a modern practical statesman. . . . Jesus was
> a first-rate political economist."[22]

Page 28 contains a set of mysterious calculations and measurements—for what?

28
2.50
14.00   87
56   72
70.00   15
34 x 69
69 ¼ x 34 ½
5 yds.

Page 29 also faces the opposite way. The following is written in a large, hurried scrawl that stops abruptly in mid-phrase.

2 Orange [?] chelack
1 pt Varnish remover
   Gold dust powder
with water alcohol
½ water ½ al
Sponge in water
Sandpaper next.
Powdered pumice stone
with crude oil—1/2 crude to rub.
strip chelacks
to fill higher
than

Pages 30–36 are out of order here. What follows are two poems, "Prayer of a Soldier in France" and "Trees" by the poet Joyce Kilmer, fighting on the Western Front, who was shot and killed by a sniper in France on July 30, 1918.[23]

Prayer of a Soldier in France.
Joyce Kilmer December 6, 1886—Aug. 1 '18 [1918]

My shoulders ache beneath my pack
(Lie easier, Cross, upon His back.)
x
I march with feet that burn and smart
(Tread, Holy Feet, upon my heart.)
x
Men shout at me—who may not speak
(They scourged Thy back and smote Thy cheek.)
x
I may not lift a hand to clear
My eyes of salty drops that sear.
x
(Then shall my fickle soul forget
The agony of Bloody Sweat?)
x
My rifle hand is stiff and numb
(From Thy pierced palm red rivers come.)
x
Lord, Thou didst suffer more for me
Than all the hosts of land and sea.
x
So let me render back again
This millionth of Thy Gift.
Amen.

<u>Trees</u>

I think that I shall never see
A poem lovely as a tree.
x
A tree whose hungry mouth is prest
Against the earth's sweet flowing breast;
x
A tree that looks at God all day,
And lifts her leafy arms to pray;
x
A tree that may in Summer wear
A nest of robins in her hair;
x
Upon whose bosom snow has lain;
Who intimately lives with rain.
x
Poems are made by fools like me,
But only God can make a tree.

Prayer During Battle
Herman Hagedorn[24]

Lord, in this hour of tumult,
Lord, in this night of fears,
Keep open, oh, keep open
My eyes, my ears.
Not blindly, not in hatred,
Lord, let me do my part.
Keep open, oh, keep open
My mind, my heart![25]

"A Little Prayer"
John Oxenham[26]

Where 'er thou be
On land or sea
Or in the air
This little prayer
I pray for thee—
God keep thee ever
Face to the light—
Thy armor bright,
Thy 'scutcheons white,—
That no despite
Thine hour smite—!
With infinite sweet oversight
God keep thee ever,
Heart's delight!—
And guard thee whole
Sweet body, soul
And Spirit high
That, live or die,
Thou glorify His Majesty;
And ever be
Within His sight,
His true & upright,
Sweet & stainless
Pure & sinless
Perfect Knight.

The evidence that in the summer of 1918 Ima Hogg was grieving for someone who died in battle is very persuasive. Why else would she copy into her little notebook those heartrending poems about death in France, death in war? What did she write on the pages she later tore out? Did Ima Hogg lose the love of her life in World War I? Scraps of evidence are tantalizing, but there is no proof. Hearsay has embroidered what might have been: Years ago, among the docents at what is now the

Bayou Bend Collection of the Museum of Fine Arts, Houston, a story circulated: "Miss Ima," as everyone called her, had had a secret romance in Germany. When her beloved was killed in World War I, she burned all his letters, but she kept in touch with his family and always visited them when she went to Germany. Others say this is just a fanciful notion.

After the war, Ima presented Mike with a leather-bound typescript edition of his wartime letters. The volume, titled *World War Letters 1914–1918*, has the initials "M.H." and "R.D." on the cover.[27] It was a gift for Mike and also for Raymond Dickson, Mike's fellow soldier and close friend. Ima, as the editor, chose the contents. There are gaps in the chronology of Mike's letters. Since none of the originals have been located, there is no way to know what may have been left out.

Ima left Dr. Foord's sanitarium in time to spend Christmas 1918 at home in Houston, but in January 1919 her depression returned. Will Hogg's diary entries, "Find Miss Ima sick abed," "Discuss Miss Ima's condition," are a bare chronicle of a trying time for the Hoggs.[28] By May 1919 Ima was in Philadelphia under the care of Dr. Francis X. Dercum, a noted specialist in mental illness. With her condition complicated by a mastoid operation in June 1919 and an appendectomy in June 1921, Ima was under Dr. Dercum's care for more than three years.[29]

In April 1923, Will, Mike, and Ima, now fully recovered, took a celebratory trip to Europe. (If Ima kept a diary, it has not been located.) The siblings sailed home separately: Will arrived in New York on the *Olympia* on June 27; Mike, on July 1 aboard the *Aquitania*. Ima came home a month later. She sailed from Hamburg, Germany, on the *Empress of Scotland*, arriving in Quebec, Canada, on August 1, 1923.[30] What she did during that time abroad without her brothers is not recorded. She returned to Europe the very next summer, sailing on the *De La Salle* from Houston in July 1924.[31]

Ima Hogg traveled to Europe again in 1926, 1929, and 1930. That year her brother Will, vacationing with her, died in Baden-Baden, Germany. Ima traveled abroad in 1935, and in 1937 she left for Europe in June and did not come home until October. Then came the turmoil that led to World War II. Ima did not visit Europe again until 1950. She continued to make regular trips abroad for the rest of her long life. Her last journey was in 1975, when she died in London at the age of 93.[32]

After all these years, Ima Hogg's secrets are still safe.

NOTES

Preface

1. James Stephen Hogg to "Editor *Chicago Record*," November 12, 1896, Box 14, Letter Press 13, pt. II, James Stephen Hogg letter transcriptions and family photographs, Woodson Research Center, Fondren Library, Rice University.

2. See Virginia Bernhard, *Ima Hogg: The Governor's Daughter*, 3rd ed. (Denton: Texas State Historical Association, 2011); Virginia Bernhard, *The Hoggs of Texas: Letters and Memoirs of an Extraordinary Texas Family, 1887–1906* (Denton: Texas State Historical Association, 2013); Kate Sayen Kirkland, *The Hogg Family of Houston: Philanthropy and the Civic Ideal* (Austin: University of Texas Press, 2009); David Warren, *Ima Hogg: The Extraordinary Cultural Patron behind the Unusual Name* (Houston: Museum of Fine Arts, Houston, 2016).

Chapter 1

1. The Hoggs did not come into their oil money from the Varner Plantation lands until 1919. Box 2J 215 and Box 3B 111, Folder: Hogg (Ima) Papers, 1824–1977; Family Papers: James Stephen Hogg: Estate records 1910–1911, Dolph Briscoe Center for American History (BCAH), University of Texas at Austin. In 1920 oil was bringing in $225,000 per month, or about $3 million in today's currency. Will Hogg to Tom Hogg, March 27, 1920, quoted in Bernhard, *The Governor's Daughter*, 66.

2. The diary is in Box 4Zg86, Ima Hogg Papers (IHP), BCAH. Ima Hogg wrote in it almost every day, noting nearly everything she saw. Since much of her diary reads like a guidebook, some sections have been heavily edited. She also bought postcards but did not mail them. There is a collection of these cards in Box 3B 153, IHP.

3. P. W. Foote, "Narrative of the 'President Lincoln,'" *Proceedings of the United States Naval Institute* 48, no. 7 (July 1922): 1073–86.

4. Records of the United States Census, 1900, 1910, 1920, Clayton Library Center for Genealogical Research (CLC), Houston; Austin College *Chromascope* 7 (1906): 101; *Houston Post*, September 11, 1908.

5. Ima's copy of the Baedeker guide has not survived. Among Ima Hogg's papers at the Museum of Fine Arts, Houston archives is a much-thumbed 1906 guidebook, Ward & Lock & Co., *Illustrated Guide Book 14*, signed by Ima Hogg. MS 21 Ser. 11 and 13, Box 15, Hogg Family Personal Papers Memorabilia Correspondence 1888–1909, Folder 13, Archives, Museum of Fine Arts, Houston.

6. David Warren's *Ima Hogg* transcribes this passage as follows: "I am really physically mentally happy spiritually and never exhausted" (61–62). The insertion of the word "happy" and transcription of "nerve" as "never" are curious alterations.

7. Mary J. Cooper is listed as the widow of Henry M. Cooper, with a residence at 1109 Elgin, in the *Houston City Directory 1907*, CLC.

8. Alexander von Fielitz (1860–1930) was a German composer. Anton Rubinstein (1820–94) was a Russian composer.

9. "Clarence Eugene Whitehill," *World Biographical Encyclopedia*, accessed January 24, 2022, https://prabook.com/web/clarence.whitehill/2512458.

10. "About: Alois Burgstaller," *DBpedia*, accessed December 23, 2021, https://dbpedia.org/page/Alois_Burgstaller.

11. Château Gütsch, built in 1888, was a luxury hotel with spectacular views of Lucerne and the surrounding mountains.

12. Ima Hogg's programs for these events are in the Ima Hogg Collection of Symphony Programs 1900–1978, University of Houston Library, Anderson/Special Collections, call no. 1969–023.

Chapter 2

1. The diary is in Box 4Zg86, IHP, BCAH.

2. In 1907 the *Berliner Adressbücher > 1900–1924* (*Berlin City Directories 1900–1924*) still list the property at Mommsenstrasse 22, Charlottenburg, as a construction site (correspondence with the archivist of the Museum Charlottenburg-Wilmersdorf in the Villa Oppenheim, Berlin, June 2015). It appears for the first time in the 1908 *City Directory*, which lists a G. Götze as the resident owner (Ima consistently uses the alternative spelling for the umlauted "o" [ö], which is "oe," i.e., Goetze). Thus, it appears that the building at Mommsenstrasse 22 was completely new.

3. Alice McFarland had arrived in Bremen, Germany, in early July. Her cablegram to her parents in Houston was reported in the *Houston Post,* July 7, 1907.

4. "Xaver Scharwenka," Naxos Records, 2021, https://www.naxos.com/person/Xaver_Scharwenka_23030/23030.htm.

Contrary to the information on the Wikipedia page about Ima Hogg ("Ima Hogg," December 12, 2021, https://en.wikipedia.org/wiki/Ima_Hogg), which was unfortunately widely accepted as correct and has therefore been propagated by numerous writers and researchers, Scharwenka was at no time court pianist to Emperor Franz Joseph I of Austria in Vienna (correspondence June 30, 2015, to February 5, 2016, with the Scharwenka Stiftung [Scharwenka Foundation] in Bad Saarow, www.scharwenka-stiftung.de). The origin of the error is unknown. Likewise, contrary to the information on the Wikipedia page, after her travels in Europe in 1907, she did not choose "to remain in Europe to continue her piano studies," and she did not study music in Vienna under Xaver Scharwenka for the next two years. As the dates in the 1907 and 1908 diaries clearly demonstrate, she went to Europe in 1907, where she traveled with friends until October 9, 1907, at which time she took a train from Florence to Berlin. She arrived in Berlin on October 10, and, after having settled at Mommsenstrasse 22, she started piano lessons with Scharwenka in Berlin until the end of January 1908, when she changed piano teachers. She lived in Berlin until October 6, 1908, the date on which she sailed from Bremen back to the United States.

5. The correct word here would have been *Bruder*, except that "oh! Brother" is not an expression used in German. Today, "Gebrüder" is used only in company names. Ima's German was still rather rudimentary. Also, the names of some of the furniture Ima lists are misspelled.

6. "Berlin," in Klaus-Dieter Alicke, *Aus der Geschichte der jüdischen Gemeinen im deutschen Sprachraum* (*From the History of the Jewish Communities in the German-speaking Countries*), 3 vols., 2014, https://www.xn--jdische-gemeinden-22b.de/index.php/gemeinden/a-b/374-berlin.

7. The programs are in a scrapbook in the Ima Hogg Collection of Symphony Programs 1900–1978, University of Houston Library, Anderson/Special Collections, call no. 1969–023.

8. Box 3B126, Folder 1, Thomas Elisha Hogg family (son of James Stephen Hogg), 1899–1970, BCAH.

9. Ima wrote "Mr. Scott" in her opera program notes from January 2, 1908. In her diary for January 2 she refers to him only as "Areal." The name in Hebrew means "lion of God." In Shakespeare's play *The Tempest,* Ariel is a spirit bound in service to the main character, Prospero. See "Ariel," Behind the Name, April 25, 2021, https://www.behindthename.com/name/ariel.

10. "August Spanuth," Schenker Documents Online, 2021, https://schenkerdocumentsonline.org/profiles/person/entity-006333.html; "Rudolph Ganz (Composer/Arranger)," Bach Cantatas Website, June 20, 2017, https://www.bach-cantatas.com/Lib/Ganz-Rudolph.htm.

11. Edward Collins, another young American studying music in Berlin, wrote of Miss Peterson, "Edna Peterson is very cute but has beaux on the brain a little." Edna boarded with the McElwees, of whom Collins says that they "are fine people and have lived in Berlin twelve years. Miss McElwee is a piano teacher. . . . There are twelve students living in their house and when they all get practicing it sounds like the Chicago Musical College." Collins lived nearby in an area that he pronounced "a great neighborhood for celebrated musicians." In his letter of August 21, 1906, he describes his lodging as "a Garten-haus room. That is, it looks into the court instead of onto the street but I like it better because it is quiet and

not so public as the front rooms." It is reasonable to assume that the Fishers had a similar arrangement. As a party of only three, plus Ima in a small spare room, it is unlikely that they occupied an apartment in the main building. See "Edward Joseph Collins: The Letters (1906–1919)," accessed December 31, 2021, http:// www.edwardjcollins.org/pdf/letters/EJC-WEB17-LETTERS-1906-19-Transcrip tionsOnly.pdf.

12. Ernst Kraus (1863–1941), a German opera singer, was appointed leading tenor at the Berlin Staatsoper in 1896, a position he held for twenty-seven years. He was much admired by Ima Hogg. See "Ernst Kraus," Deutsche Digitale Bibliothek, accessed December 31, 2021, https://www.deutsche-digitale-bibliothek. de/person/gnd/116387483.

Baptist Hoffmann (1864–1937), a German baritone, was engaged at the Berlin Royal Opera House from 1897 to 1910. See "Baptist Hoffmann (Baritone)," Forgotten Opera Singers, March 19, 2015, http://forgottenoperasingers.blogspot. com/2015/03/baptist-hoffmann-baritone-1864-1937.html.

13. Paul Knüpfer (1866–1920) was a German bass opera singer at the Berlin Royal Opera House, remembered for having taken part in the disastrous premiere of Ruggero Leoncavallo's *Der Roland von Berlin* (1904). See "Overview: Paul Knüpfer (1866–1920)," Oxford Reference, 2021, https://www.oxfordrefer ence.com/view/10.1093/oi/authority.20110803100041191.

Kurt Sommer (1868–1921) was a German tenor who became a member of the Berlin Court Opera in 1893, where he remained until his death. He was memorable for singing in the Berlin premieres of *Die Meistersinger* and *The Flying Dutchman*. See "Kurt Sommer," Forgotten Opera Singers, July 19, 2014, http://forgottenoper asingers.blogspot.com/2014/07/kurt-sommer-tenor-altengottern.html.

Frieda Hempel (1885–1955) was a German-born American coloratura soprano whose operatic performances made her one of the leading singers in the world. See "Hempel, Frieda (1885–1995)," Encyclopedia.com, 2019, https://www .encyclopedia.com/women/encyclopedias-almanacs-transcripts-and-maps/ hempel-frieda-1885-1955.

Richard Strauss (1864–1949) was a German composer (no relation to the Austrian Johann Strauss family famous for their waltzes) and chief conductor of the Berlin Royal Court Opera from 1898 to 1908. His composition *Notturno* premiered in Berlin on December 3, 1900, with the composer conducting the Berlin Philharmonic and with baritone Baptist Hoffmann (1864–1937), who was then at the beginning of his twenty-two years with the Berlin Opera. See Michael Kennedy, "Richard Strauss: German Composer," *Britannica*, accessed January 24, 2022, https://www.britannica.com/biography/Richard-Strauss. Accessed January 24, 2022.

14. Dante Michaelangelo Benvenuto Ferruccio Busoni was an Italian composer, pianist, music teacher, and conductor. See "Ferruccio Busoni (Composer/ Arranger)," Bach Cantatas Website, June 14, 2017, https://www.bach-cantatas .com/Lib/Busoni-Ferruccio.htm.

15. See "Émile Sauret (1852–1920)," Naxos Records, 2021, https://www.naxos.com/person/Emile_Sauret/23348.htm.

Felix Senius (1868–1913) was a German tenor who became one of the most important concert tenors of his time. See "Felix Senius," Forgotten Opera Singers, September 14, 2019, http://forgottenoperasingers.blogspot.com/2019/09/felix-senius-tenor-konigsberg-germany.html.

16. See "Josef Lhévinne," Naxos Records, 2021, https://www.naxos.com/person/Josef_Lhevinne/2229.htm.

17. Leopold Godowsky (1870–1938) was one of the most highly regarded pianists of his time, heralded as the "Buddha of the Piano." He was the teacher of many famous pianists. See "Leopold Godowsky," Steinway & Sons, 2021, https://www.steinway.com/artists/leopold-godowsky.

18. Bronislaw Huberman (1882–1947) was a renowned Polish violinist and founder of the Palestine Orchestra. When Ima heard him, he was exactly her age. See "Orchestra of Exiles," PBS, 2021, https://www.pbs.org/wnet/orchestra-of-exiles/star-violinist-who-saved-jews-before-the-holocaust/; and "Bronislaw Huberman," Rob Huberman's Website, 2021, http://bronislawhuberman.com.

19. A Bedag was the commonly used name for an electric taxicab of the Berliner Elektromobil-Droschken Aktien-Gesellschaft (BEDAG).

20. Melanie Kurt (1880–1941) was an Austrian soprano who became internationally known through her guest performances on both sides of the Atlantic. See Laura Wagner-Semrau, "Melanie Kurt," Opera Vivra, 2011–2021, http://www.operavivra.com/artists/sopranos/melanie-kurt/.

21. See "Onkel Toms Hutte," Architects, December 31, 2021, http://architectuul.com/architecture/onkel-toms-hutte.

22. Folder I-1–37, Ima Hogg Photographs Collection, BCAH. Hartmann, like Ima Hogg, lived in Charlottenburg.

23. Edouard Risler was a noted French pianist and champion of modern composers. See "Edouard Risler," Naxos Records, 2021, https://www.naxos.com/person/Edouard_Risler/43885.htm.

Joseph Joachim was a well-known Hungarian violinist, composer, and teacher who had died in August 1907. See "Joseph Joachim," *Britannica*, accessed December 31, 2021, https://www.britannica.com/biography/Joseph-Joachim. Karl Halir, a Czech violinist, was a student of Joachim's.

Henri Marteau, a French violinist and composer, became head of the violin department at the Royal Hochschule of Berlin. See "8th International Violin Competition: Henri Marteau," Hofer Symhoniker gGmbH, accessed December 31, 2021, https://www.violinwettbewerb-marteau.de/en/home.html.

24. Mark Hamburg (1879–1960) was a Russian-born pianist. See "Mark Michailovich Hamburg," *Prabook*, 2021, https://prabook.com/web/mark.hamburg/3740219.

25. Arthur M. Abell was a critic for the *Musical Courier* in Berlin during 1895–1907.

26. Literally, Goetze boy; however, considering the news he related, it is unlikely that Ima referred to Siegfried's little brother Gerhard. She may mistakenly have thought that Goetze Junge was the equivalent of Goetze Jr., i.e., Siegfried.

27. Eugène Ysaÿe (1851–1931) was a Belgian violinist, composer, and conductor who in his day was regarded as "The King of the Violin." See "Eugene Ysaÿe," *New World Encyclopedia*, August 12, 2017, https://www.newworldencyclopedia .org/entry/Eug%C3%A8ne_Ysa%C3%BFe.

Emanuel Moor, a Hungarian composer, was not particularly admired, as the review in the *New Music Journal* of the performance Ima Hogg attended demonstrates. According to the critic, the applause was given to Ysaÿe, the nonpareil among violinists, but even he was unable to make Moor's Concerto palatable. See "Neue Zeitschrift fuer Musik 1908 Jg75 zugl MW Jg39," Internet Archive, accessed December 31, 2021, https://archive.org/stream/NeueZeitschriftFuer Musik1908Jg75ZuglMwJg39/NeueZeitschriftFuerMusik1908Jg75ZuglMwJg39_ djvu.txt.

Johann Svendsen (1840–1911) was a Norwegian composer, conductor, and violinist who became the leading Scandinavian conductor of his day. See "Johann Svendsen (1840–1911)," Naxos Records, 2021, https://www.naxos.com/person/ Johann_Svendsen/23858.htm.

Henryk Wieniawski (1835–80), a Polish violinist and composer, was one of the most celebrated violinists of the nineteenth century, regarded as the "reincarnation of Niccolò Paganini." See "Henryk Wieniawski," *Britannica*, accessed December 31, 2021, https://www.britannica.com/biography/Henryk-Wieniawski.

28. Thila Plaichinger (1868–1939) was an Austrian soprano. From 1900 to 1914 she was a soloist of the Berlin Hofoper. See "Thila Plaichinger," Mahler Foundation, accessed December 31, 2021, https://mahlerfoundation.org/mahler/ contemporaries/thila-plaichinger/.

Wilhelm Grüning (1858–1942), like Paul Knüpfer, also participated in the disastrous premiere of Ruggero Leoncavallo's *Der Roland von Berlin*.

Marie Goetze (1865–1922) was a German contralto known for performances in operas by Richard Wagner. See "Marie Goetze," Great Singers of the Past, February 18, 2018, https://greatsingersofthepast.wordpress.com/2018/02/18/ marie-goetze-contralto/.

Hermann Bachmann (1864–1937) was a German operatic baritone, opera director, and singing teacher. See "Hermann Bachmann," Wikipedia, March 7, 2021, https://en.wikipedia.org/wiki/Hermann_Bachmann.

Putnam Griswold (1875–1914) was an American bass-baritone who was highly admired as a Wagnerian. He made his operatic debut at Covent Garden in London and continued his training in Paris, Frankfurt am Main, and Berlin. See "Griswold, Putnam," Encyclopedia.com, 2019, https://www.encyclopedia.com/ arts/dictionaries-thesauruses-pictures-and-press-releases/griswold-putnam.

29. Thomas W. Dixon's *The Leopard's Spots* (1902) was the first of his trilogy of novels romanticizing the Ku Klux Klan after the Civil War.

30. Marie Corelli was a popular novelist in the 1890s. *The Master Christian* (1900) follows the career of a humble man who becomes a Roman Catholic cardinal.

31. Lewyn began her career as a concert pianist in Germany in 1909 to considerable acclaim. See Michael Duke, "Movers and Shakers, 1909," *Jewish Herald Voice* (Houston), May 31, 2007.

32. See "Artur Schnabel: 1882–1951," Schnabel Music Foundation, accessed December 31, 2021, https://schnabelmusicfoundation.com/musicians/artur-schnabel.

33. Giuseppe Tartini (1692–1770) was an Italian Baroque composer, violinist, and theorist credited with establishing the modern style of violin bowing. See "Giuseppe Tartini," *Britannica*, accessed December 31, 2021, https://www.britannica.com/biography/Giuseppe-Tartini.

Henry Vieuxtemps (1820–81) was a Belgian violinist and composer. See "Henry Vieuxtemps (1820–1881), Naxos Records, 2022, https://www.naxos.com/person/Henry_Vieuxtemps/22380.htm.

34. Ema (Emmy) Destinn (1878–1930) was a Czech soprano and a recognized interpreter of the works of Mozart, Wagner, and the Italian opera, as well as of Czech works. See "Emmy Destinn," *Memim Encyclopedia*, 2021, https://memim.com/emmy-destinn.html. Could Ima possibly have meant Francis Maclennan (1873–1935)? See "Francis Maclennan," Forgotten Opera Singers, April 23, 2012, http://forgottenoperasingers.blogspot.com/2012/04/francis-maclennan-bay-city-1873-port.html. In *Die Musik* for 1907–8, a semimonthly music magazine, a "Herr Maclennan" is mentioned as having "here [the Royal Opera House] already sung Radames after Caruso." Caruso had sung the role of Radames in October 1907 and, according to Emil Ledner, Caruso's German manager in Berlin, "the applause stopped the show. . . . What happened at the end of this [final] duet [with Emmy Destinn] was not merely applause, but an uproar, a cry of jubilation. The audience clapped, and stamped their feet." See "Die Musik," Internet Archive, accessed December 31, 2021, https://archive.org/stream/bub_gb_rmw5AAAAIAAJ/bub_gb_rmw5AAAAIAAJ_djvu.txt; and "Anecdotes," Enrico Caruso, 2010, https://www.enricocaruso.dk/index-18.html. In the review of the current event, no specific date given, the critic compares Maclennan's performance to the tenor's earlier performance at the Royal Opera House, perhaps the one on February 10, 1908, that Ima Hogg attended, and gives him a very favorable review, saying that he has made great progress in singing, in mastering the German language, and in expressing the dramatic content of the opera.

35. Sandra Droucker (1875–1944) was a Russian Jewish pianist and teacher who taught at the Stern Conservatory in Berlin for several years. She was an advocate of the Schenkerian theory. See "Sandra Droucker," Schenker Documents Online, 2021, https://schenkerdocumentsonline.org/profiles/person/entity-000175.html.

36. See "Martin Krause," Wikipedia, December 23, 2021, https://en.wikipedia .org/wiki/Martin_Krause.

37. Augusta (Gussie) Zuckermann (1887–1981) was an American pianist and composer who studied under Leopold Godowsky and Busoni in Berlin. She was a musical prodigy. When only seven years old, she played at Carnegie Hall. She adopted Mana-Zucca as her stage name and pseudonym. See Lindsay Conway, "Mana-Zucca," Library of Congress, March 11, 2021, https://blogs.loc.gov/ nls-music-notes/2021/03/american-composers-and-musicians-from-a-to-z-x-z-part-1-zwilich-ellen-taaffe-and-mana-zucca/. For a detailed description of her colorful life, see "AMICA International Honor Roll," AMICA Automatic Musical Instrument Collectors' Association, accessed December 31, 2021, https://www .amica.org/files/Mana-Zucca.pdf.

38. Emma Calvé (1858–1942) was a French opera singer celebrated for her role as Carmen.

39. Arthur Nikisch (1855–1922), a Hungarian conductor, was considered one of the finest conductors of the late nineteenth century. See "Arthur Nikisch," *Britannica*, accessed December 31, 2021, https://www.britannica.com/biography/ Arthur-Nikisch.

Ossip Gabrilowitsch (1878–1936), a Russian-born American pianist, was noted for the elegance of his playing. See "Ossip Gabrilowitsch," *Britannica*, accessed December 31, 2021, https://www.britannica.com/biography/Ossip-Salomonovich-Gabrilowitsch.

40. Ima needed papers allowing her to reside in Germany. "Mr. T." was probably Lewis Thompson, her 1907 tour companion, who helped with the documentation.

41. Ima's grandfather was Colonel James Stinson, at whose country home Ima had spent many happy days. Her youngest brother, Tom, was then serving in the US Marine Corps.

42. Ima had evidently been wearing mourning colors since her father's death: black for the first year; then in the second year, with the mourner in half-mourning, softer colors such as gray, mauve, and some shades of purple were the custom and suitable for that time. See Dolores Monet, "History of the Mourning Dress: Black Clothing Worn during Bereavement," Bellatory, April 9, 2021, https://bellatory. com/fashion-industry/FashionHistoryMourningDressBlackClothingWornDur ingBereavement; and Lou Taylor, *Mourning Dress: A Costume and Social History* (Boca Raton, FL: Routledge, Taylor and Francis Group, 1983), https://www.rout ledge.com/Mourning-Dress-Routledge-Revivals-A-Costume-and-Social-History/ Taylor/p/book/9780415556545.

43. Muzio Clementi (1752–1832), an Italian-born British composer and pianist, was called the "Father of the Piano." See "Muzio Clementi," *Britannica*, accessed December 31, 2021, https://www.britannica.com/biography/Muz io-Clementi.

44. Tom Hogg to Ima Hogg, Box 3B126, Folder 1, BCAH.

45. Box 4Zg86, IHP, BCAH.

46. Box 4Zg86, IHP, BCAH.

47. For Norway heritage data, see "SS Kaiser Wilhelm der Grosse, Norddeutcher Lloyd," Norway-Heritage: Hands across the Sea, accessed December 31, 2021, http://www.norwayheritage.com/p_ship.asp?sh=kaiwi.

48. *Houston Post*, December 16, 1908; May 30, June 9, and October 3, 1909.

49. Bernhard, *The Governor's Daughter*, 54–55; Warren, *Ima Hogg*, 68–70.

50. Nettie Jones, interview by Virginia Bernhard, Houston, November 20, 1979; Mary Fuller, interview by Virginia Bernhard, Houston, 1980.

Chapter 3

1. *Houston Post*, June 29, 1910.

2. The "Exhibition" was a World's Fair: Exposition Universelle et Internationale de Bruxelles. No wonder Mike and Ima had a hard time finding rooms. If they had been there two weeks later, they would have witnessed a very destructive fire. However, ultimately the fire probably contributed to the huge number of visitors that came to the event: thirteen million. See "Belgian Exposition Is Wiped Out by Fire," *New York Times*, August 15, 1910, https://www.nytimes.com/1910/08/15/archives/belgian-exposition-is-wiped-out-by-fire-gale-sweeps-flames-over.html.

3. The "Earl and Countess" were Sir Francis Greville, Fifth Earl of Warwick, and his wife, Lady Frances Evelyn.

4. Ima meant that they went by trolley to the Milverton railway station, not to the town of Milverton, which was 150 miles away.

5. *Houston Post*, January 28, 1912.

6. *Waco* [Texas] *Morning News*, March 25, 1912; and *Galveston Daily News*, March 29, 1912. On Ima Hogg and the Episcopal Church, see Warren, *Ima Hogg*, 72–73.

7. For Rouse, see *Houston City Directory 1908*; *Houston Post*, September 20, 1908; US Census of 1910, CLC. For Laura Franklin, see US Census of 1900 and 1910, CLC.

8. Galveston Index to Passengers 1906–1951, Reel 2, M-1358, Drawer C43, D 10, CLC.

9. On Ima's key role in the founding of the Houston Symphony, see Kirkland, *The Hogg Family of Houston*, 167–73; Carl Cunningham, Terry Ann Brown, and Ginny Garrett, *Houston Symphony: Celebrating a Century* (Houston: Houston Symphony Society, 2013); and Warren, *Ima Hogg*, 73–78.

Chapter 4

1. Will Hogg, Diary 1914, Diaries 1913–1915, Box 2J398, William Clifford Hogg Papers, BCAH.

2. Barbara Tuchman's *The Guns of August* (New York: Macmillan, 1962) is the classic account of the beginning of the Great War.

3. Hoek van Holland is a small coastal town in the Netherlands. Ferries to England have operated there since 1893.

4. Ima was on an English ship with a Russian name. The SS *St. Petersburg* was built in 1910 for the Great Eastern Railway. Renamed *Archangel* in 1916, used as a cross-channel troop ship, and acquired by the London and North Eastern Railway in 1923, it was bombed and sunk on May 16, 1941, off the east coast of Scotland. See "Great Eastern Railway," 1999–2010, http://www.simplonpc.co.uk/LNER_GER1.html.

5. The *Chemnitz* was built in 1901 for North German Lloyd. On June 6, 1914, it left Bremen on its last voyage to New York, Philadelphia, and Galveston and was then laid up in Bremen in August 1914 for the duration of the war. In 1919 the ship was surrendered to Britain and scrapped in Holland in 1923. See "Passenger Manifest of the S.S. Chemnitz," Our Family History, 2001–22, http://familytree.ghzis.com/showmedia.php?mediaID=810&medialinkID=3722.

6. Mary Elizabeth Rouse and Ruth Curtis had evidently been Ima Hogg's travel companions aboard the *Chemnitz*. Rouse taught piano in Houston in the early 1900s, and she was one of Ima Hogg's companions on a trip to Europe in 1911. About Ruth Curtis, nothing is known. *Houston City Directory 1907* and *1913*, microfiche FC01D08, CLC; *Houston Post*, September 20, 1908; Box 3T240, I 68, Ima Hogg Photograph Collection, BCAH.

7. James W. McClendon, an attorney from Austin; his wife, Anne; and their two young daughters, Mary Anne, age five, and Elizabeth, age four, had been aboard the *Chemnitz*. *City Directories of the United States*, 043002, Austin, 1912–1914, microfilm, CLC; United States Fourteenth Census (1920), CLC.

8. Ima may have seen this item in the London *Daily Mirror* on August 4, 1914: "The Daily Mirror's Paris correspondent states that before Baron von Schoen, the German Ambassador, left Paris he told Monsieur Viviani that Germany considered herself in a state of war with France, and the reason for it was because French airmen had dropped bombs on Nuremberg." See Virginia Bernhard, ed., "Ima Hogg in Europe, 1914: A Texan Experiences the Beginning of the Great War," *Southwestern Historical Quarterly* 119, no. 3 (January 2016): 278n.

9. American-born Kitty Cheatham had an international career as a popular entertainer. See Bernhard, "Ima Hogg in Europe," 278n.

10. Fritz Kreisler, the Austrian violinist and composer, served only briefly. He was wounded and honorably discharged in 1914. See "Fritz Kreisler," Legendary Violinists, accessed December 31, 2021, www.thirteen.org/publicarts/violin/kreisler.html.

11. Sir Edward Grey served as Foreign Secretary of the United Kingdom from 1906 to 1916. He said, looking out his office window the evening before his August 4, 1914, speech: "The lamps are going out all over Europe; we shall not see them lit again in our lifetime." See Bernhard, "Ima Hogg in Europe," 278n.

12. Olive Schreiner was a well-known South African author and antiwar activist. See Bernhard, "Ima Hogg in Europe," 278n.

13. Arthur James Balfour, Prime Minister of the United Kingdom from 1902 to 1905, was a Conservative Party leader. In 1915 he succeeded Winston Churchill as First Lord of the Admiralty. See "Arthur James Balfour, 1st Earl of Balfour," *Britannica*, accessed December 31, 2021, http://www.britannica.com/biography/ Arthur-James-Balfour-1st-earl-of-Balfour. Horatio Herbert Kitchener, military commander and diplomat, was the United Kingdom's Secretary of State for War in 1914. See Bernhard, "Ima Hogg in Europe," 280n.

14. Mary Smith had evidently been one of Ima's travel companions aboard the *Chemnitz*.

15. Constance Collier (1878–1955) was a famous English stage and film actress. See Bernhard, "Ima Hogg in Europe," 281n.

16. Mrs. Greg (Grey?) Leavell was evidently an American traveler staying at the Imperial Hotel, stranded, like Ima and others, by the war.

17. No wonder Ima's passengers were nervous: "The basic technique of punting is to shove the boat along with a pole by pushing directly on the bed of the river or lake. . . . The normal approach was for the passengers to sit at the stern on cushions placed against the till, and for the punter to have the run of the rest of the boat. The punter started at the bow, planted the pole, and then walked towards the stern, shoving the punt forwards. This is known as 'running' the punt." See "Punt (boat)," Wikipedia, November 21, 2021, en.wikipedia.org/wiki/ Punt (boat).

18. Arthur Rackham (1867–1939) was a famous English book illustrator. See "Arthur Rackham: 1867–1939," Tate, accessed January 24, 2022, https://www .tate.org.uk/art/artists/arthur-rackham-1811.

19. The stained-glass windows were the work of artists Edward Burne-Jones and Ford Madox Brown and designer William Morris in the 1870s. See Bernhard, "Ima Hogg in Europe," 284n.

20. Arthur Tooth & Sons was a famous London art gallery founded in 1842. See "Archives Directory for the History of Collecting in America," The Frick Collection, accessed December 31, 2021, http://research.frick.org/directoryweb/ browserecord.php?-action=browse&-recid=6419>.

21. Promenade Concerts have been part of London summers since 1895. In 1914 they were held at Queen's Hall, Langham Place, Westminster. Sir Henry Wood was one of the series founders. See "Henry J. Wood (Conductor, Arranger)," Bach Cantatas Website, May 30, 2017, www.bach-cantatas.com/Bio/Wood-Henry .htm.

22. Percy Grainger (1882–1961) was an Australian-born composer and pianist. He and Ima Hogg were the same age. See "Grainger, George Percy (1882–1961)," *Australian Dictionary of Biography*, 2006–22, http://adb.anu.edu.au/biography/ grainger-george-percy-6448-.

23. Jessie Brett Young, the soloist, was the wife of the British physician and novelist Francis Brett Young. See Leslie Gilbert Pine, *Who's Who in Music* (London: Shaw Publishing, 1915), 320.

24. Solomon Cutner, a child prodigy from London's East End, was twelve years old when Ima heard him play. See Bruce Eder, "Solomon," AllMusic, 2021, http://www.allmusic.com/artist/solomon-cutner-mn0001786746/biography.

25. Russian forces had invaded East Prussia on August 17, 1914. See Bernhard, "Ima Hogg in Europe," 287n.

26. Rowena Teagle was evidently a New York friend from Ima's days as a music student in that city in the early 1900s. Rowena and her husband lived in New York and had been leasing a country house in England that summer. United States Fourteenth Census (1920), CLC.

27. Herbert Asquith was Prime Minister of the United Kingdom from 1908 to 1916. See "Herbert Asquith," History.com, updated August 21, 2018, http://www.history.com/topics/british-history/hh-asquith-1st-earl-of-oxford-and-asquith. In 1914 Winston Churchill was First Lord of the Admiralty. See "Churchill's First World War," Imperial War Museums, 2021, www.iwm.org.uk/history/churchills-first-world-war.

28. Canadian-born statesman Bonar Law was leader of the Conservative Party in 1914. See "Andrew Bonar Law," Spartacus Educational, 1997–2020, http://spartacus-educational.com/PRbonar.htm.

29. "Mrs. Royse" was obviously English. Whether she was a pension guest or an employee is not clear.

30. Philip Snowden was a prominent antiwar member of the Labour Party. See "Philip Snowden," Spartacus Educational, 1997–2020, http://spartacus-educational.com/REsnowden.htm.

31. The battle of Mons, fought on the border between France and Germany on August 23, 1914, was the first major action of the British Expeditionary Force (BEF). A victory for the Germans, the battle cost the BEF sixteen hundred casualties. See Bernhard, "Ima Hogg in Europe," 290n.

32. Ima's reference to 177 is to the policeman they had met at the rally. In Ima's eyes, he was as much a hero as Mrs. L.'s historical heroes.

33. Frederich von Bernhardi was a German general whose 1911 book argued for war as a "biological necessity" in accord with nature's law. See "Bernhardi," *WWI Biographical Dictionary*, July 15, 2009, http://wwi.lib.byu.edu/index.php/Bernhardi.

34. Mrs. Wiggs was a character in a popular 1901 novel, *Mrs. Wiggs of the Cabbage Patch.*

35. See "New York, U.S., Arriving Passenger and Crew Lists, 1820–1957," Ancestry.com, 1997–2021, search.ancestry.com/search/db.aspx?dbid=7488.

36. Mike Hogg's letters home are in Virginia Bernhard, ed., "A Texan in the Trenches: Mike Hogg's World War I Letters," *Southwestern Historical Quarterly* 117 (July 2013): 49–67 (part 1), and (October 2013): 164–81 (part 2).

Chapter 5

1. *Houston Post*, May 15, 1918; Kirkland, *The Hogg Family and Houston*, 172–73; Warren, *Ima Hogg*, 88–90.

2. This was the Lake Placid Club, founded in 1895, in Lake Placid, New York. Warren, *Ima Hogg*, 89.

3. Most of the pages are fully reproduced here to serve as a record of Ima Hogg's extraordinary diligence in collecting antiques, in guiding the Houston Symphony, and in constantly improving her mind.

4. A search for individual names has been fruitless, but the Springfield Economy Rug Company is listed in Massachusetts Bureau of Statistics, *A Directory of Massachusetts Manufactures, 1913: Classified by Industry; Corporation, Individual, or Firm Name; and Location*, reprint, March 3, 2018, https://www.amazon.com/Directory-Massachusetts-Manufactures-1913-Corporation/dp/0243100566. Ima Hogg's notes are reprinted here in full as a record of her interest in antiques and early adventures as a collector.

5. Bernhard, *The Governor's Daughter*, 10.

6. Ima Hogg, "Pocket Notes," Box 4Zg86, 26, IHP, BCAH.

7. Quilts are mentioned in Mrs. Gilbert H. Spooner's advertisement in *Antiques*, December 1922, 296a. Nichols & Stone, the oldest wood-furniture building company in the United States, closed in 2008 after 151 years. See *Furniture Today*, June 16, 2008. Ima's note about "82 Logan" is probably a memo about an address on Logan Street in Boston. The Brooklyn Chair Company was advertising in 1918. See https://www.periodpaper.com/products/1918-ad-brooklyn-chair-co-bedroom-chairs-furniture-original-advertising-069099-gf2-246.

8. Mike Hogg to Ima Hogg, undated note; Mike Hogg to Ima Hogg, September 23, 1918, Box 3B125, Family Papers, IHP. If Mike wrote once a week to his sister, many of his letters are missing.

9. Mike Hogg to Ima Hogg, June 15, 1918, Box 3B125, IHP.

10. Mike Hogg to Ima Hogg, June 23, 1918, Box 3B125, IHP.

11. Mike Hogg to Ima Hogg, July 8, 1918, Box 3B125, IHP.

12. Ima's illness is evident from Will Hogg's diary entries of July 20–22 and August 1 and 8, 1918, Box 2J399, Will Hogg Papers, BCAH.

13. Was Ima mourning the loss of someone she knew from her time in Munich in 1907 or her 1908 year in Berlin? Siegfried Goetz, Leola's husband, did not die in the war. Neither did "Buddy," Leola's brother, nor Charles Scott, aka "Areal."

14. Edward Prather to Will Hogg, July 29, 1918, Box 3B119, Folder 1, IHP, BCAH.

15. The camp, built around 1910 by Russell Spinney, still exists. Today it is called Tomhegan Cabins. See "Tomhegan Wilderness Camps," in George Smith, *Maine Sporting Camps* (Lanham, MD: Rowman and Littlefield, 2016), 189, https://www.google.com/books/edition/Maine_Sporting_Camps/K0JKDAAAQBAJ?hl=en&gbpv=1&dq=Tomhegan+Cabins,+Maine&pg=PA189&printsec=frontcover.

16. Nathaniel Bartlett Sylvester, *The History of Ulster County, New York* (Philadelphia: Everts and Peck, 1880), 2:60.

17. J. George Frederick, "Reconstructing American Business," *The Dial*, October 19, 1918, 294–97. The *Dial* was a literary and political magazine published intermittently from 1844 to 1929.

18. Mary Fisher, *Journal of a Recluse* (New York: T. Y. Crowell, 1909), 189.

19. Robert W. Service, novelist and poet, served as an ambulance driver for the French in World War I. See "Robert W. Service," Poetry Foundation, 2022, http://www.poetryfoundation.org/bio/robert-w-service.

20. This is paraphrased from Walter E. Weyl, *The End of the War* (New York: Macmillan, 1918).

21. Ima Hogg probably read this poem in Robert W. Service's *Rhymes of a Red Cross Man* (New York: Barse and Hopkins, 1916), 11, a book of war poems dedicated to his brother, who was killed in World War I.

22. Frank Harris, "Bernard Shaw and Jesus the Christ," *Pearson's Magazine*, November 1916, 429. The quotation's ellipsis is Ima Hogg's. She had obviously read the entire essay, but she was mistaken about its being a letter that Shaw wrote to the magazine. It was an article by Frank Harris, a journalist. *Pearson's* was a magazine of literature, the arts, and politics, published from 1899 through the 1920s. See "Pearson's Magazine," Online Books Page, accessed December 31, 2021, http://onlinebooks.library.upenn.edu/webbin/serial?id=pearsonsusa.

23. Kilmer wrote these poems in France while he was serving in the war. See "Joyce Kilmer," Poetry Foundation, 2021, http://www.poetryfoundation.org/bio/joyce-kilmer; and "Remembering Sergeant Joyce Kilmer (1886–1918)," December 28, 2014, https://genemcvay.wordpress.com/tag/prayer-of-a-soldier-in-france/.

24. Hermann Hagedorn was an American biographer/poet. See "Hermann Hagedorn," Wikipedia, September 15, 2021, https://en.wikipedia.org/wiki/Hermann_Hagedorn.

25. For text of the poem, see "Hermann Hagedorn: Prayer during Battle," Infoplease, updated February 28, 2017, http://www.infoplease.com/t/poetry/modern-verse/prayer-during-battle.html.

26. John Oxenham's book of inspirational verses, *The Fiery Cross: Some Verses for To-Day and To-Morrow*, was published in 1917. See https://books.google.com/books?id=4yVCAQAAMAAJ&pg=PA4&lpg=PA4:&dq=%22A+LIttle+Prayer%22+John+Oxenham&source=bl&ots=EJWqyS0kuM&sig=plD5ar0U7Azf_PYf-VLhlXeNOvI&hl=en&sa=X&ved=0ahUKEwjS0Z7pmfjLAhUQ-GMKHeswB54Q6AEIITAB#v=onepage&q=%22A%20LIttle%20Prayer%22%20John%20Oxenham&f=false.

27. *World War Letters 1914–1918*, Hogg Family Personal Papers, MS 21, Hogg Family Papers, Museum of Fine Arts Archives, Houston.

28. For an account of Ima's illnesses, see Will Hogg's Diary, April 1919 to April 1923, passim, William Clifford Hogg Papers, BCAH.

29. Bernhard, *The Governor's Daughter*, 59–60.
30. "New York, U.S., Arriving Passengers and Crew Lists, 1820–1957."
31. Passenger lists in Genealogical Research Files, CLC.
32. Bernhard, *The Governor's Daughter*, 1–2.

Index